AMERICA'S BEST
RIBS

AMERICA'S BEST
RIBS

Tips and Recipes for Easy, Lip-Smacking, Pull-off-the-Bone, Pass-the-Sauce, Championship-Quality BBQ Ribs at Home (Plus a Few Ribilicious Sides and Desserts)

Ardie A. Davis, PhB, and

Chef Paul Kirk, CWC, PhB, BSAS

Andrews McMeel
Publishing, LLC
Kansas City • Sydney • London

Andrews McMeel Publishing, LLC
an Andrews McMeel Universal company
1130 Walnut Street, Kansas City, Missouri 64106

www.andrewsmcmeel.com

12 13 14 15 16 WKT 10 9 8 7 6 5 4 3 2 1

ISBN: 978-1-4494-1413-9

Library of Congress Control Number: 2011932660

Book design by Diane Marsh

Rib illustrations by Jen McClure

Photography by Jonathan Chester, Extreme Images: 68, 120, 123; and by Selma Dakota, Extreme Images: xii, 20, 47, 84, 100

Food preparation by Paul Kirk, KC Baron of Barbecue, and Jason Day, Burnt Finger BBQ

ATTENTION: SCHOOLS AND BUSINESSES
Andrews McMeel books are available at quantity discounts with bulk purchase for educational, business, or sales promotional use. For information, please e-mail the Andrews McMeel Publishing Special Sales Department: specialsales@amuniversal.com

For Robert Ian Carruthers
December 15, 1947, to April 24, 2011

Our friend and barbecued-rib aficionado!

Con-tents

DANGER

RIBS ARE DDICTIVE

B DOCTOR

Intro-duction

**E**ver since Adam decided he could "spare" one, ribs have played an important role on our planet. While we're sure that Eve was indeed a beauty of a rib, she would have been hard-pressed to top the beauty of the Grand Champion award-winning ribs at the Jack Daniel's World Championship Invitational Barbecue each year. Ribs connect us to our primal core, like the hunters gathered by the fire, hunched over and happily grunting and chomping away at a Fred Flintstone–sized brontosaurus rib. Ribs, especially barbecued ribs, stir primal passions in carnivores, omnivores, and recovering vegetarians and vegans alike. They are perhaps more popular than any other barbecued meat, as they are easier to eat, easier to cook, and delicious, and may be the one common meat found at all barbecue joints everywhere. Thankfully, that ready availability means we no longer need to chase down a mastodon to get our barbecue fix, but when it comes to making ribs at home, some people seem to be intimidated.

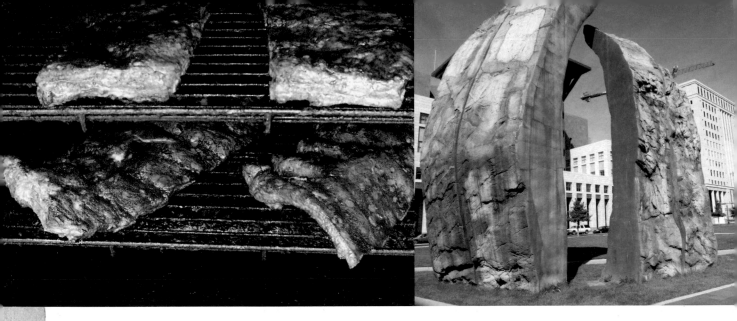

Ardie's good friend Stan Nelson shared a story about a reunion of Stan's former air force buddies in Aix-en-Provence, France. Stan said, "About fifty pilots and their wives were invited to a wine tasting at the French Air Force Academy. It was a lovely afternoon spent at a long table under some trees. On the table were eight or so bottles of French wines separated by trays of finger foods. People crowded around the table, but not being that interested in wine, I stood back, next to a French pilot who had been in my flight class. I told him I presumed he also was not that interested in wines. He corrected me and said, no, he had a wine cellar of about a thousand bottles, and he recorded the characteristics of many of his wines annually to determine whether age improved them. I asked him about those characteristics, and in a casual manner he launched into the subject and spent considerable time on wine complexity—that feeling about a wine that comes minutes or longer after the wine is swallowed. Looking for the bottom line, I asked, 'In your years of studying and quantifying the characteristics of wines, what factors make the best wine?' He smiled and said, '*The best wine is the wine you like.*"

We know some barbecue aficionados who can match wine or cigar connoisseurs with the complexity of their rib talk. One bite of a rib and they can tell you what breed of animal it came from; the age, gender, and diet of the animal; its grazing *terroir*; its last meal; and how and where it was killed and processed. Then they'll tell you how it was cooked—the fuel, the seasonings, the wood smoke, the length of time—and sometimes they'll tell you who cooked it! Don't be intimidated. They may know all that about a rib, or maybe they're blowing smoke. It comes down to this: *the best rib is the rib you like*! Our goal in writing this book is to help you cook your personal best ribs, whether they're country style, loin, or baby backs.

So how can you trust us to deliver the goods on America's best ribs? We wish we could claim that ribs have been our favorite food since infancy—that we teethed on rib bones and ate blended ribs from a baby food jar before we could chew. That's almost true. We each have fond memories of rib enjoyment dating back to childhood. Grilled ribs or ribs slow roasted in the oven with barbecue sauce—or, on special occasions, slow-smoked ribs from a local barbecue joint—sustained us through our early years. Then, more than three decades ago, we got involved in competition barbecue, where pork ribs smoked slow and low are the ultimate ribs.

WE LIKE THE WHOLE MAINSTREAM RIB SPECTRUM— PORK, BEEF, BISON, LAMB, AND MUTTON.

Paul, a.k.a. the Baron of Barbecue, is now a professional chef, restaurateur, and winner of more than five hundred barbecue awards, including seven world championships. Ardie, also known as Remus Powers, PhB, founded the Diddy-Wa-Diddy National Barbecue Sauce Contest in 1984, which spawned the American Royal International Barbecue Sauce, Rub, & Baste Contest, as well as the Great American Barbecue Sauce, Baste, and Rub Contest. He is a longtime backyard barbecuer and a barbecue historian, and since he doesn't compete in contests, Team Remus is undefeated. Between the two of us we bring more than a hundred years of experience with barbecue, including barbecued ribs, and we have judged more contest ribs over the years than many people eat in a lifetime. Trust us.

Although our first choice in ribs is lightly seasoned pork spares (it's what we grew up with, smoked slow and low), we like the whole mainstream rib spectrum—pork, beef, bison, lamb, and mutton. We've focused on those most popular ribs cooked with tried-and-true recipes instead of obscure meats and cooking techniques. If you want recipes for fish ribs, alligator ribs, or other exotics, you won't find them here. While we love ribs that are oven-roasted, fried, or slow cooked in a crock, the recipes here are for smoked and

grilled ribs, since that's our area of expertise. In our own cooking we draw the line at using aluminum foil or boiling ribs before throwing them on the cooker, so you won't find those in this book, either. What you will find are seventy-five recipes that range from basic, traditional, American classics to more adventurous flavor fusions. They represent a cross section of American food culture, including Korean, Chinese, European, and Indian flavors. Many are marinated or rubbed, some are glazed and sauced, others are served dry, and we even cover brining, so we hope they'll give you a variety of techniques to experiment with.

We offer you some recipes that have garnered awards in contests, as well as recipes that have made people shout, "This is a winner!" The proof, however, is in *your* eyes, *your* nose, and *your* palate. Regardless of the honors a rib cooked with a championship recipe has garnered, it can fall short of what you like. This applies to ribs that have been given maximum scores by all who judged them. Remember: The best rib is the rib you like. And half the fun is in what you learn along the way. With that in mind, Chapter 1 contains enough tips and tricks to help you branch out, experiment, and develop your own best rib recipe, whether you're a well-seasoned competitor or a passionate weekend barbecuer.

As much as we would like to believe that man can live on ribs alone, we have to admit that we like a good side with our ribs, so we're throwing in some of our favorite sides that we think complement ribs well. For our previous book, *America's Best BBQ*, we traveled far and wide in our search for America's best barbecue, so the sides here also represent a variety of regional favorites. And since no meal is complete without a sweet finish, we're also including some of our favorite finales for a feast of ribs.

Whether you like your ribs sweet or spicy (or both), sassy, dry or sauced, minimalist or well-seasoned, tangy, savory, grilled or slow-smoked, there's something here for everyone to put together a memorable rib feast. Without further ado, it's time to make some of America's best pull-off-the-bone ribs and some ribilicious sides and desserts. So grab some Wet-Naps, pass the sauce, and dig in!

CHAPTER 1

Rib
Basics

A comment often heard around barbecue pits is, "I taught her everything she knows, but I didn't teach her everything I know." Nevertheless, barbecuers are some of the friendliest, sharingest people you'll meet. They like to swap cooking secrets, and when they're proud of something they've cooked, don't be surprised if they offer you a morsel. Just don't expect them to teach you everything they know. The X-factor is very much alive in barbecue culture.

Ribs—even cheaper cuts—are an investment, and you want to protect your investment against waste. You can waste your ribs by how you cook them—burned to a crisp, for example—but another waste risk is how you select, prep, and season your ribs. This chapter includes not only some basic information for selecting, prepping, and seasoning your ribs, but also some tips on the equipment and notes on fuel, cooking techniques, and testing for doneness. After that you can stick with the basics or try your hand at more complicated techniques and flavor profiles—some of which may astound your judges, whether they be competition officials or backyard rib aficionados, and a few of which may flop—but each new experiment is another step on your way to becoming a ribmaster.

Barbecuers are an open-minded, food-loving group, and they're generally open to ideas and love to try other styles of cooking, from braising to roasting to slow cooking and frying. That said, we're focusing on grilling and smoking in this book because those are the two most popular cooking styles for ribs and even in cookbooks we like to think that the "write what you know" rule applies. You can certainly use many of the rubs, marinades, and sauces in your favorite baked and slow-cooked rib recipes, too. Just remember that as in grilling and smoking, low and slow is the best way to get tender, delicious ribs.

All cooks stand on the shoulders of cooks who came before them. While the recipes here come mostly from Paul, he's often influenced and inspired by others. And while his has been a very successful way, it's not the only way. We hope you'll take everything we say with a grain of salt—be it kosher, sea, celery, onion, garlic, or your own particular taste—and put your stamp on it. You are the ribmaster. Own that attitude, and the techniques you learn here will put you in the company of championship ribmasters.

Buying Ribs

Today's rib market is packed with a good variety of choices—from cheap, big, and tough to tender, smaller, and more expensive. Quality and price don't mean everything. The bottom line is how the ribs taste, and the method of cooking has everything to do with making great ribs. Bad cooking can ruin good ribs, and good cooking can make bad ribs fabulous. For a good example, read Phil Litman's story about John Willingham's championship ribs in Cleveland, Ohio, on page 116.

As a rule, supermarkets, national membership discount clubs, and many butcher shops carry ribs from mass-production meat processing plants. If you're just looking to cook everyday ribs at home, slabs from the mainstream marketplace are fine for the recipes in this book. They are more affordable and in line with the barbecue tradition of transforming cheap, tough meat into mouthwatering feasts. Unfortunately, you're often at a disadvantage in seeing the ribs, since they're in a package—most likely Cryovac, maybe even packed two to three slabs per package. They're also often frozen. You'll just have to do your best, or else go to a butcher to be absolutely sure what you're getting.

If you're looking to take your ribs to the next level, any accomplished ribmaster, backyard barbecue queen or king, or contest champion will tell you to get to know a butcher or meat cutter. Meat cutters worth their salt know enough about all kinds of ribs to guide you to the best available. (One way to ensure this would be to bring them samples to show how you're progressing and get further tips. A sample might be enough—but a meal might get you farther!) With experience, you'll learn how to find and select the ribs that will work best for you, though it is still important to be on a first-name basis with your local butchers or meat cutters. The meat industry is constantly changing, and you can keep up to date through your contacts on the front line.

Bison ribs may be a little tougher to find. First, check with your local meat distributors and butchers. You might be surprised at what they can get. If not, good bison ribs are available online (see Resources).

Selecting Ribs

First some general rules, followed by a few specific ones.

Does price matter? Yes and no. In general, quality goes up as price goes up, but again, the cooking method can make all the difference.

Fresher is better. There are times when aged meat is preferred, but when we're selecting ribs, the fresher the better. Freshness is especially important with pork and lamb; less so with beef.

Buy according to the occasion. Know your guests and know your limits. Know where your guests are from, what they like or don't like, and their intake capacity. Always overestimate on their appetites, however, as people who like ribs will eat more than usual.

If you're pressed for time, get loin or baby back ribs and grill them. Guests from Memphis will expect a choice of wet (sauced) or dry (just rubbed) ribs. Texans will want lightly seasoned (with salt and pepper) or unseasoned slow-smoked dry ribs with barbecue sauce or hot sauce on the side—and given their druthers, spareribs will be preferred over baby backs. The bottom line is, you're the pitmaster and host, but while we always say, "The best ribs are the ribs you like," it doesn't hurt to figure out what your guests like and keep them coming back.

Tips for Selecting Ribs

1. **Size of the slab**—For pork ribs, the smaller the slab, the younger the hog and the smaller the bones, which means that the meat-to-bone ratio is better. Baby backs are sold by weight. True baby back (or loin back) slabs weigh 1¾ pounds or less, though many stores sell bigger ones. For spareribs, "4.9 and down" in meat terminology are considered "light ribs," and 5 pounds and up are "medium ribs." A full slab of pork spareribs should have about 12 rib bones. Country-style ribs are sold by weight, rather than size or number.

    For beef and bison ribs, look for short ribs that have 3 or 4 ribs per slab and back ribs that have 7 bones per slab. Short ribs are normally cut to the size the store or butcher wants to sell, and you can ask the butcher or meat cutter to cut them again to the size you need. For back ribs, don't be fooled by the smaller number of bones—your slabs will be plenty big, about 10 by 15 inches. Bison ribs will be a bit bigger.

    Lamb ribs (also called *lamb breast ribs*) and mutton ribs have 12 ribs per slab. Denver ribs (see page 88) have 7 ribs. Lamb ribs are more tender than mutton, but many people enjoy mutton because it has a stronger flavor.

2. **Meaty, but marbled**—this goes for all types of ribs. There should be bits of fat (marbling) running through the meat. Look for fat that is intertwined in the meat, not in big globs. See page 7 for information on removing excess fat.

3. **No shiners (exposed bones)** on your pork (baby backs and spareribs), beef and bison short ribs, and lamb and mutton ribs. This is harder to apply for beef and bison backs, which are mostly shiners these days.

Prepping Your Ribs

You can cook your ribs primal style without prepping them first, but prepping your ribs is quick and easy, and it gives you a better-looking, juicer, and better-tasting finished product. The steps here apply to all of the types of ribs covered in this book. For additional information on prepping St. Louis–style ribs, see page 24.

Trimming Off the Skirt

The skirt is a flap of meat on the bony side of the ribs. Skirts vary from narrow to wide depending on how much was left when the animal was butchered, and skirts usually have a piece of the diaphragm attached to them, which should always be cut off. Chef Paul likes to cut off the whole skirt, but it's optional.

To remove the skirt, place a sharp knife against the bones beneath the skirt and slice it off in one piece parallel to the bones. Strip off the diaphragm and membrane (see Skinning Your Slab, page 6) and discard them, but save the meat.

Skinning Your Slab

There is a thin, tough, rubbery membrane on the bone side of the slab. Most restaurants don't remove it because doing so is more labor-intensive. If you are hanging your slabs in a smoker, you want to leave it on because it helps support the weight of the slabs. However, ribmasters usually remove it for two reasons: Removing it maximizes the power of your seasonings, and guests or judges prefer not to munch on the membrane. Experienced ribmasters have skinned so many slabs over their lifetime that they make it look easy. With practice and persistence you'll make it look easy, too.

Removing the membrane is a two-step procedure. First, insert a clam or oyster knife, or the handle of a metal eating utensil, beneath the membrane on the slab end opposite the skirt end. Pointed handles work best. In a pinch, you could even use a Phillips-head screwdriver. Lift up enough membrane to grab hold of it.

Next, use a paper towel or dish towel to grip the membrane and peel it off. If you're lucky, it will come off in one piece. If not, it might tear, and you'll have to peel it off in pieces.

You'll notice another membrane below the one you've peeled off. It isn't tough, and you needn't bother with removing it. If you do, the bones will fall out.

Leave the Fat on, or Scrape It off?

If you leave the fat, it will render off during cooking, but your rub will work better if some of the fat is scraped off before cooking, and you'll have less trouble with flare-ups if you're grilling over direct heat. Use a dinner spoon to scrape off some of the fat that was under the membrane. The dull edge won't cut into the remaining membrane or meat. You may also want to trim some of the fat from the meaty side of the slab. Use a sharp boning or paring knife, but be gentle and avoid cutting all the way to the bone, lest you end up with shiners (exposed bone).

Outlining Beef and Bison Ribs

Beef and bison ribs have a tough secondary membrane on the bone side, so we like to outline the back of the ribs (about ¼ inch deep) with a sharp, pointed paring knife so that we can get more seasoning into the meat. This is not necessary for other types of ribs.

Cut the Ribs into Serving Portions Before You Cook Them, or Leave Them Whole?

Some recipes here tell you to cut up the ribs before you cook them, though most don't. It's usually a lot of unnecessary work, though sometimes you can't avoid it because the size of your cooker won't accommodate the size of your slabs. Some people like to roll the ribs like a jelly roll to fit their cooker (or to fit more in their cooker), like the ones in the illustration here, but that blocks smoke from getting to all the surface area of the meat. If necessary, cut your ribs into as few pieces as possible to fit your cooker.

Room-Temperature Ribs

Remove your ribs from the refrigerator at least 1 hour before cooking them to let them come to room temperature. If you remove them just before you heat your cooker, by the time it reaches the desired temperature the ribs should be close to room temperature.

Rib Rubs

A rub is a dry spice or a combination of dry spices, from just salt and pepper to any concoction you can dream up to season whatever you are going to smoke or grill. Like marinades, they add flavor to your meat before you cook it. Normally you season with dry rubs before cooking, not during or after.

Rib rubs have become as expected a part of a ribmaster's repertoire as a hammer to a carpenter. In competition circles, not using a rub is akin to being a heretic in religion. You could be excommunicated—or judged down! That said, rubs are personal, and the decision to use a rub is personal. While we prefer them over marinades and brines, we don't always use them, and the recipes in this book are a mix of rubbed and marinated styles so you can experiment with each.

When Chef Paul teaches how to build rubs in his pitmaster classes, he recommends balance, such as between salt and sugar. They are flavor enhancers as well as flavor carriers for the spices, herbs, and other components you add. It's best to use like-sized granules of salt and sugar and use smaller amounts of powdered spices and herbs. This way everything mixes well and stays in suspension for more even seasoning.

Try experimenting with different sizes of seasonings. Large grains, such as kosher salt or turbinado (raw) sugar, don't give you very good coverage. Powders, such as garlic powder, can give you a much better finished product, but when you add enough to cover the meat their flavor can become very strong. But garlic salt, for example, gives you both good coverage and a well-seasoned product. The salt carries the flavor of garlic.

Moisture, light, and heat aren't good for rubs, so store them in a cool, dry, dark place. They'll keep for 2 to 3 months that way or for up to 6 months in the freezer. We like to put our rub in a clean plastic shaker bottle to make it easy to store and use.

MORE ISN'T BETTER, EXCEPT SOMETIMES, WHEN IT IS.

When putting together ingredients for rubs or sauces, Chef Paul generally sticks to the rule that less is better. When you start adding herbs or spices to basic flavor carriers such as salt or sugar, it is easy to get carried away and add too much of a good thing. Either you end up with something that tastes mysterious and awful, or you've gone to a lot of trouble to end up with an indistinct, blah flavor that won't even work as fish bait.

However, one of Chef Paul's pitmaster students from Ethiopia once proved wrong that general rule. True to his upbringing, his rub had enough different spices in it to fill a spice specialty shop. Paul was sure it would turn out to be a hodgepodge of flavors that canceled each other out and would totally overpower the natural flavor of a barbecued rib, but those darned ribs turned out to be the best in the class!

Because rubs are such a critical part of our own rib prep, we're going to get you started with four flexible proven winners from the Baron's master-class repertoire. If you'd like to experiment with marinades, bastes, brines, and sauces, look to the recipes in the chapters. Each ingredient list is separated into the basic components so you can easily pull out a component and try it somewhere else.

BARON'S BASIC BARBECUE SPICE

Makes about 1 cup

This is a great all-purpose rub that works well with all meats. It has served Chef Paul (a.k.a. the Baron of Barbecue) well in hundreds of contests.

6 tablespoons paprika

3 tablespoons dried light brown sugar (see page 11)

2 tablespoons dry mustard

1½ teaspoons granulated garlic

1½ teaspoons ground celery seeds

1½ teaspoons sea salt

1½ teaspoons ground thyme

1½ teaspoons ground coriander

1½ teaspoons ground marjoram

¾ teaspoon cayenne

Combine all the ingredients in a small bowl and blend well. Store in an airtight container in a cool, dry place for 2 to 3 months or in the freezer for up to 6 months.

WHAT KIND OF SALT IS BEST?

While some of our recipes use kosher, flaked, or sea salt, they're not always ideal because of the size of the granules, which can be too large to create adequate coverage. Chef Paul prefers flavored salts such as seasoned salt, garlic salt, onion salt, celery salt, and the like so he gets the benefit of the extra flavor.

He doesn't always favor plain salt (either iodized or noniodized) because of the flavor. Try this experiment: On a small plate, place a teaspoon of kosher salt, a teaspoon of sea salt, and a teaspoon of plain salt in separate areas. Taste them in that order. They are all the same chemical formula—NaCl—but the plain salt will taste bitter compared with the kosher and sea salts because it's mined from the ground, and therefore often contains mineral and other residues, and iodized salt has iodine added.

When cooking competition ribs, Chef Paul stays away from iodized salt because the iodine could cause your meat to turn out splotchy. Otherwise it's fine for home use. (Tip: A little paprika serves to enhance the color of your competition ribs.)

SWEET RIB RUB

Makes about 1¾ cups

Use this rub on smoked ribs or as a finishing seasoning on grilled ribs. Don't grill over direct heat with this rub. The sugar will burn.

1 cup white cane sugar

½ cup Baron's Basic Barbecue Spice (page 9)

¼ cup seasoned salt

½ teaspoon ground allspice

¼ teaspoon ground ginger

⅛ teaspoon ground cloves

Combine all the ingredients in a sifter and sift into a bowl to blend well. Store in an airtight container in a cool, dry place for 2 to 3 months or in the freezer for up to 6 months.

BASIC TEXAS RIB RUB

Makes ¾ cup

A lot of people think a rub should be complicated. Not so. This is used in many parts of Texas. It's easy—and it works.

¼ cup salt

¼ cup paprika

¼ cup freshly ground black pepper

Combine all the ingredients in a small bowl and blend well. Store in an airtight container in a cool, dry place for 2 to 3 months or in the freezer for up to 6 months.

SASSY TEXAS RIB RUB

Makes about 1 cup

There isn't any sugar in this smooth blend of spices, but there's enough cayenne to sass you with a wallop. In true Texas fashion, you could use it on goat, or cabrito. Unfortunately, we don't have any recipes for goat ribs here, so you could use it on just about anything.

⅓ cup salt

¼ cup paprika

3 tablespoons chili powder

2 tablespoons freshly ground black pepper

1 tablespoon ground cumin

1 tablespoon granulated garlic

1 tablespoon cayenne

Combine all the ingredients in a sifter and sift into a bowl to blend well. Store in an airtight container in a cool, dry place for 2 to 3 months or in the freezer for up to 6 months.

Applying the Rub

For best results, pat the ribs with a paper towel before applying the rub. Lightly sprinkle the rub on all exposed parts of the slab. The bony side will absorb about half as much rub as the meaty side will. You can stop with that, or if you want more rub flavor, wait 10 minutes and apply a second coat. Although it is called a rub, you needn't literally rub it into the slab. Some cooks do. We don't. We think packing it on smothers the ribs—keeping the smoke out—and the results aren't as good.

Reseasoning the Ribs

Some cooks put their ribs in the smoker as soon as they're rubbed. That's what we prefer, because it's less hassle and it draws out less moisture from the meat. Others wait an hour or more while their plastic-wrapped ribs soak up seasonings in a cooler or refrigerator. If you let the rubbed ribs sit for a few hours or overnight, reseason them just before cooking to freshen up the flavor.

CANE SUGAR VS. BEET SUGAR VS. BROWN SUGAR

You may notice that the recipes that call for granulated sugar specify white cane sugar. Chef Paul's mother, grandmothers, and even a great-great-grandmother always swore that cane sugar was a better flavor enhancer than beet sugar, and while he has no scientific proof to back up that claim, he thinks it does taste better. In general, cane sugar granules are also smaller than beet granules, and he likes that for the same reason he favors fine salt. That said, nothing is wrong with using beet sugar, which is a common sugar. The majority of people can't tell the difference, and you can make a fantastic and an award-winning rub using either sugar!

We rarely call for brown sugar in a rub, because it clumps, but when we do, we dry it. Some brown sugar is white sugar with molasses or cane syrup added (the darker the sugar, the more molasses). Don't substitute Demerara or turbinado (raw) sugar. Those aren't the same thing, and they have large granules and higher melting points.

DRYING BROWN SUGAR FOR USE IN RUBS

In a large mixing bowl, combine 1 pound of light brown sugar and ¼ cup of cornstarch and mix with an electric mixer on low speed until fully incorporated. Turn the speed to medium to medium-high and mix for 3 to 5 minutes. Store in a tightly sealed container in a cool, dry place.

Marinades

A marinade is a liquid mixture usually composed of an acidic ingredient, such as vinegar, wine, or fruit juice, and a more neutral one, such as water or oil, along with various spices and herbs. You soak your meat in it before cooking. Chef Paul considers it a flavor enhancer, and some say it makes meat more tender by beginning to break down and tenderize the fibers in the meat. Marinades are particularly important and useful in grilling because the high, intense heats can dry out your meat.

The acid in marinades helps protect meat from the formation of harmful bacteria, but it is no excuse to ignore the rules of safe food handling. Always marinate meat in the refrigerator to prevent bacteria from forming, and do not baste meat with used marinade that has not been boiled for at least 2 to 3 minutes to kill any harmful bacteria.

When we marinate ribs, we like to place them in a large (2-gallon) resealable plastic bag, add the marinade, seal the bag tightly (letting all the air out), and gently turn the bag to make sure the entire rib surfaces are coated with the marinade. You can also marinate the ribs in a large, covered rectangular baking dish. Just make sure they're well coated.

You could marinate for less than an hour or up to 24 hours. The longer the marinade stays in contact with the meat, the stronger the flavor.

FROM A SIGN AT A POPULAR RIB JOINT IN NEW YORK: "'VEGETARIAN' . . . INDIAN WORD FOR 'LOUSY HUNTER'"

Brines

At its most basic, brine is a solution of water and salt, though some brines include sugar and other spices. You may need to heat the brine in order to dissolve the seasonings, but cool it to room temperature before using it so that the hot brine doesn't begin to cook the meat. Meat is soaked in brine in the refrigerator for varying lengths of time, based on the size of the cut. Brined meat is more moist and flavorful than meat that has not been brined. After you remove ribs from brine, rinse them to remove excess salt, then pat dry. You may also want to reduce the amount of salt in your rub.

Sops, Mops, and Bastes

Sops, mops, and bastes all are basically the same thing. Back in the old days, before we were barbecuing, the meat had a tendency to dry out. So our forebears concocted a flavorful liquid to apply to the dry meat. They dipped clean rags in the liquid and sopped it on the meat. Then came the dish mop to apply the liquid, so it was a mop. Now we just call it a baste, and most of us apply it using a garden mister so we can adjust the spray.

You may want to use either straight apple juice or a mixture of half apple cider vinegar and half apple juice to help retain moisture during cooking. We prefer apple juice, which won't change the flavor of the meat. Try both ways and make your own decision. Either of these bases also works well to put down flare-ups.

Many of the recipes in this book recommend serving your ribs with the remaining sop, mop, or baste. We like to do so because it keeps the flavor profile consistent, though you may prefer to serve your ribs with another sauce. There is some risk of exposure to bacteria when serving the remaining sop, mop, or baste, so for safety's sake, place the remainder in a saucepan, bring it to a boil, and let it cook for 1 to 2 minutes before serving.

Sauces and Glazes

A sauce is a seasoned liquid barbecue condiment. Popular bases are tomato, vinegar, and mustard; soy sauce, mayonnaise, pureed fruit, and other things are also used.

A glaze is basically a sauce brushed on the meat as it finishes cooking. You can make it yourself, or it can be as simple as a store-bought barbecue sauce that you brush on a slab of ribs during the last 30 minutes of the cooking process. Some combine their barbecue sauces with a light honey, such as clover, or another sweetener such as brown sugar or agave, usually in a 2:1 ratio (2 barbecue sauce to 1 sweetener).

As with sops, mops, and bastes, you can serve the remaining sauce with your ribs, and the risk of exposure to bacteria is lessened, since the ribs usually have been cooking quite awhile before you glaze them with sauce. However, it's not totally risk-free, so if you have any concerns, boil the sauce for 1 to 2 minutes before serving.

Equipment

Long-handled tongs, basting mops and brushes, spatulas, and **heavy-duty oven mitts** are useful for tending foods while cooking. **Spray bottles** are good for both basting and taming flare-ups. It's also a good idea to keep an **ABC fire extinguisher** handy, just in case.

A **grill thermometer** is a handy tool. An easy way to modify your grill to fit one is to take a wine cork and drill a hole the diameter of your thermometer through the middle of the cork from top to bottom. Fit the cork into one of the top grill vents, and push the thermometer through the hole in the cork. That way you can constantly monitor the internal temperature and your thermometer won't touch the metal of the grill, which could give you an inaccurate reading.

Many people recommend using a **meat thermometer** to test for doneness. It's tough to do that for some types of ribs, but it works well on others. For more, see page 19.

A **drip pan** can be a helpful accessory for indirect cooking, though you may not bother with one if you don't mind the mess. The pan should be large enough to cover the surface below the ribs. Place the pan on one side of the cooker and use long-handled tongs to arrange coals on the other side of the cooker. You can buy a disposable aluminum pan or improvise one using a sheet of heavy-duty aluminum foil about 2½ times as large as the food you will be cooking. Fold the foil in half; then fold up the edges to make 2-inch-high sides. Crease the corners to seal.

A **water pan** is useful for smoking. You can make your own by taking an aluminum bread pan (or larger size), placing it in the bottom of your cooker next to the coals, and pouring water into the pan to fill it.

A **chimney starter** is helpful for cooking with charcoal. You just stuff the bottom with paper, turn the chimney over, put it on the fire grate, fill it with briquettes (around ninety-two in a standard chimney), and set the paper on fire. The fire then moves to the coals, and once the coals are ash gray (20 to 30 minutes), you use a fireproof glove or mitt to grasp the chimney handle and dump the hot coals on one end of the fire grate.

Many cook ribs flat on the grates of their cooker. Some professional and competition cookers, like Chef Paul, hang their ribs while they smoke. **Rib racks** like the ones shown here are becoming more popular because they let you cook more slabs at once. Ardie likes to use those.

Direct vs. Indirect Cooking

Direct cooking is a method of quickly grilling food by placing it on a rack directly over the heat source. It is often done uncovered on a charcoal grill but covered on a gas grill. It is faster than indirect cooking because more intense heat is applied, and it allows for browning the outside of foods.

Indirect cooking is a method of grilling slowly, to one side of the heat source, over a drip pan in a covered cooker. Hot air circulates around the food, much like in a convection oven, and it cooks more slowly because less heat is provided. We like this method best for ribs, and we actually think it's easier than direct grilling because you don't have to turn the meat as

often, but we understand that sometimes you want something quicker. Each recipe title notes whether the ribs are grilled over direct heat or smoked over indirect heat.

Which Is Better: Cooking with Gas vs. Cooking with Charcoal

Many people prefer to use gas grills because of speed and convenience, but we prefer to use charcoal because of the flavor it imparts to the meat. Of course, you can add wood to either one to enhance the flavor of the meat, as well. Here is a basic rundown of the differences between using gas and charcoal, but you'll want to consult your own manual for further instructions.

Cooking with Gas

You will want to refer to your owner's manual for specific directions for direct and indirect cooking on a gas grill. In general, for indirect cooking on a two-burner gas grill, after preheating with both burners, you will turn off one burner and place the food over the unlit side, away from the heat source. For three-burner gas grills, you will turn off the middle burner after preheating and place the food in the center of the grill. Ribs are juicy, so use a drip pan. You can set the ribs on a rack in a roasting pan and the roasting pan on the grill rack.

Cooking with Charcoal

You can buy two different kinds of charcoal. Charcoal briquettes made of compacted ground charcoal, coal dust, and starch are most common. They come in standard and easy-lighting forms. Easy-lighting briquettes are pretreated with a lighting solution for a quick start and need to burn for only 10 minutes before they are ready for grilling. They can be a real time-saver, but we don't recommend them because they can lend a petrochemical flavor to your meat. You also can use lump charcoal—the carbon residue of wood that has been charred, usually in the form of lumps. Refer to your manufacturer's directions for setting up and lighting your charcoal grill.

It's harder to monitor and regulate the temperature of charcoal grills than that of gas grills. You can monitor temperature with a thermometer in the lid vent hole (see page 14), and you can maintain your desired temperature by controlling oxygen intake to coals by adjusting the bottom vent holes. More air means faster, hotter cooking. Less air allows for slower cooking.

If you're direct grilling with an uncovered grill, charcoal briquettes will burn for 40 to 45 minutes as a general rule. If you leave the lid on, most kettle grills will hold a steady temperature of 225° to 275°F for at least 6 hours of smoking. When you must lift the grill cover, lift it to the side rather than straight up—otherwise suction may draw ash onto the food.

To keep the grill going for several hours, you'll probably need to add more charcoal. It's best to add hot coals instead of fresh briquettes. Just before you put the grill grate over your first batch of coals, remove two and place them in the bottom of a chimney starter. Then fill the chimney starter with fresh briquettes and set it aside on a heatproof surface, such as concrete or bricks (not asphalt), so that it can preheat while you put your meat on the grill. By the time you need to add more coals to your fire, the coals in the chimney should be preheated and ready to go. Repeat as needed.

Woods for Smoking

Natural wood chips and chunks can be added to a fire to impart a smoky flavor to food as it cooks. Alder, apple, cherry, hickory, maple, mesquite, oak, and pecan are commonly used. The chips are soaked in water for about an hour, drained well, and added to a fire just before putting food on the grill. In kettle grills or gas grills, water-soaked wood chips or dry smoke pellets work best. For charcoal cookers, just dump them on top of the hot coals or flames. For gas grills, place the soaked chips in heavy-duty foil, make a package, seal the edges, poke holes in the top, and place the package on the hot burner or lava rock. Use tongs to remove and dispose of the package afterward when cool. Large cookers with a firebox on the side take well to wood logs or chunks. Follow your manufacturer's directions.

We encourage the use of the hardwoods available locally. In the Pacific Northwest, that would be alder. In the Midwest and South, hickory, pecan, and oak. In the Southwest, mesquite. In the Northeast, maple. Also check for availability of fruit woods such as apple, peach, cherry, and pear in your area. If you're partial to a certain wood that isn't local, barbecue woods of any variety can be shipped worldwide from a variety of suppliers (see Resources, page 135).

"BARBECUED RIBS": ASK BEFORE YOU ORDER

When "barbecued ribs" are on the menu of a place that doesn't specialize in real barbecue, ask a few questions before ordering.

1. How were the ribs cooked? Smoked, charcoal-grilled, gas flame–grilled, boiled, oven-baked, or cooked in a crockery slow cooker? Sometimes "barbecued" does not mean that they actually were barbecued, as in smoked. It just means they've got barbecue sauce on them.

2. If not specified, are the ribs pork, beef, or other? If pork, are they spares, loin, or country style? If beef, long or short? If other, what other and what cut?

3. If you decide to order the ribs, ask for sauce on the side. Otherwise they may be drowned in barbecue sauce, as in the photo here.

(WE ATE THEM ANYWAY.)

We've had some bad, disappointing ribs at some nonbarbecue restaurants and some tender, tasty nonbarbecue ribs in nonbarbecue restaurants. Truth is, when you're not the cook, ordering ribs in a restaurant is a game of chance.

Guidelines for Grilling Ribs

Grilling should be done over direct heat at medium to medium-high temperatures. Use long-handled tongs to spread the coals evenly in a single layer. Extend them about 1 inch beyond the area of the ribs and make sure you leave a cool zone on the other side of the cooker. Turn the ribs frequently as they cook, about every 5 to 10 minutes depending on the meat (see individual recipes) and how hot your fire is. If the ribs are caramelizing, turn more frequently. If flare-ups are intense, move the ribs to the cool zone to allow fat in the fire to burn down, then continue to grill in the hot zone. Rotate the ribs occasionally to evenly cook them.

Guidelines for Smoking Ribs

Smoking should be done over indirect heat at between 225° and 275°F for between 3½ and 6 hours. It's not an absolute science. The suggested times given in the recipes in this book are just estimates, and your actual cooking time might vary quite a bit based on your type and brand of cooker, the outside and inside temperatures, and the cut of ribs. The best way to check doneness is by the look and feel of the meat, or in the case of beef or bison short ribs or country-style pork ribs, with a meat thermometer. When smoking, it doesn't hurt to err on the side of cooking longer, because keeping it low and slow means more tender meat. And an extra 30 minutes isn't likely to burn or ruin your ribs.

Unlike for grilled ribs, don't check them often, because you'll lose heat and time. Chef Paul likes to turn them at half times. For example, if your total cooking time is 4 hours, turn them 2 hours in, then again in another hour, then in 30 minutes. Always start bone side down and baste each time you turn. As with grilled ribs, rotate the ribs when you turn them for more even cooking.

General Tips for Cooking Ribs

- The temperatures given in our recipes are the temperatures your cooker should be preheated to before you put the meat on.

- The cooking times we give are estimates. Your time will vary depending on the type and weight of the meat and your cooker's ability to hold the heat.

- When lighting your grill, remember to divide your cooking space into a hot zone and a cool zone, whether you're cooking with gas or charcoal, or over direct or indirect heat.

- Your grate should be 3 to 6 inches above the coals or flames. The closer it is to the flames, the more carefully you'll have to watch your meat and handle flare-ups.

- Always lightly coat your clean grates with a little bit of oil or nonstick cooking spray.

- Don't leave your cooker unattended while it's lit.

Avoiding Flare-Ups

When you're cooking over direct heat, sometimes meat juices drip into the coals, briquettes, or rocks, causing flare-ups that can burn your meat. Flare-ups can wreck a great meal in seconds, so always be on the lookout, especially when grilling over direct heat.

To avoid flare-ups when barbecuing, place the meat opposite the hot coals, briquettes, or rocks. This creates a cool zone so that you can move meat back and forth from flames to cool zone as necessary. Trimming excess fat from the meat also helps prevent flare-ups. You can also try lowering the heat by raising the grill rack and spreading the coals so there is more space between them. Or you can remove some of the coals or cover the grill.

For excessive flare-ups in a charcoal grill, you may need to remove the meat from the grill and mist the flames with a water-spray bottle.

Do not mist flare-ups on a gas grill. Simply close the lid and wait for the flare-up to die down. Some lava rock systems can collect grease that may result in flare-ups, so be especially watchful when using them and change them once a season if you use your grill a lot. When you open your propane tank valve, it might help to turn it only one turn so that you can turn it off in a hurry in the event of a flare-up.

Once the flames die down, you can return the food to the grill and resume grilling.

Testing Ribs for Doneness

For ribs, anything over 140°F is OK. It's difficult to test most ribs for doneness with a meat thermometer because there's just not much to work with, and getting the thermometer close to a bone will throw off your reading. We recommend using a thermometer for beef short ribs (which should read 185°F when done), and you could use it on country-style pork ribs (140°F or higher), too. You also can pull on or slice country-style pork ribs to check their tenderness.

Beef and bison backs, pork baby backs and spares, and lamb and mutton ribs are done when you can take two side-by-side ribs and pull them apart and the meat pulls away from the bones.

When the meat reaches the desired doneness, remove it from the cooker and let it stand for 10 to 15 minutes before cutting or serving to let the juices redistribute.

CHAPTER 2:

Pork Ribs

BABYBACKS, COUNTRY STYLE, and SPARERIBS

KC was a potbellied pig who lived his entire life as the housemate of Gary and Carolyn Wells, founders of the Kansas City Barbeque Society. He was the official KCBS mascot when Gary and Carolyn officiated at barbecue contests. When KC died, he was mourned by his many fans and was given a proper burial in Gary and Carolyn's backyard. There are pigs you share your life with and there are pigs you eat.

As national livestock expert Mike Lake, PhB, of Lynch Livestock Company, told us, the commercial swine-production industry today includes all kinds of breeds. What started with a few purebreds like Danish Landrace, English Large White, Hampshire, Duroc, Yorkshire, and Chester White hogs has developed into a field full of hybrids of all sorts, many selected for size and weight. You'll never know what breed you're getting at the store, or at many butcher shops, for that matter, so some people have taken to buying their own hogs or buying shares of a whole hog. Any pork works well in the recipes in this book, but don't forget to review our selection tips on page 4.

In North Carolina, if it isn't pig it isn't barbecue. Although we don't agree with that pigheaded hogma, we have a great appreciation for pig barbecue—whole hog, shoulder, ham, jowls, snout (pronounced "snoot," for those in the know), or ribs—and especially ribs. And we're not alone.

Since pork ribs are the most popular ribs in America, this is the longest chapter in the book. Pork ribs can be grilled, smoked, boiled, braised, roasted, and fried. Here you'll find recipes for grilling and smoking—heavier on the smoking, since we believe that's the best way to cook moist and tender ribs. We stand fast in our opposition to boiling or foiling, so none of the recipes call for those methods. Before we get into the recipes, here are a few tips on the types of pork ribs. For information on selecting and prepping all types of ribs, see Chapter 1.

Types and Cuts of Pork Ribs

Baby back (or loin back) ribs, from the upper section of the rib cage near the spine, are smaller, meatier, and the easiest of the three to cook. The term is often applied to any size slab of loin back ribs, but true baby backs are 1¾ pounds or less.

Country-style ribs are not allowed in barbecue competitions because they aren't really ribs. John Scavuzzo of Scavuzzo's meat company and S&S Meats (where Paul buys most of his ribs by the case) pointed us toward a definition from *The Meat Buyer's Guide*, put out by North American Meat Processors (NAMP). Basically, it said that country-style ribs are cut from the shoulder end of a bone-in pork loin, and they should have 3 to 6 ribs, divided into equal portions. So while country-style ribs are not true ribs, we're including them here because a lot of people don't know that, and they find them pretty tasty (and convenient) just the same. We're willing to overlook where they come from as long as they are delicious.

One of the pitfalls of grilling any rib, but especially country-style ribs, is having too hot a fire. Country-style ribs shouldn't be treated like a steak—grilled hot and fast. You don't want them raw inside. Stick to lower heats than you'd use for a steak and have that cool zone ready.

Spareribs, from the lower breast bacon (belly) section of the pig, often are less meaty and are a less expensive cut than baby backs. They may come with costal cartilages and with or without the brisket bone (breastbone) removed and the diaphragm trimmed. A slab should have 11 or 12 ribs. Light slabs weigh 4.9 pounds or less. Medium slabs weigh more than 4.9 pounds.

Pork Ribs

St. Louis–Style Pork Ribs

While the recipes in this chapter use baby backs, country-style ribs, and full slabs of spareribs, we know a lot of people like St. Louis–style ribs, and you can substitute them for spareribs in any recipe without altering the cooking time.

St. Louis–style ribs are pork spareribs that have been trimmed of the rib tips and skirt meat. While St. Louis–style slabs are smaller than full sparerib slabs, and therefore closer to the size of baby backs, they are more meaty and more forgiving than baby backs. A lot of people prefer them because their size tends to be more consistent than full, untrimmed spareribs, so they look more formal and cook more evenly. Trimming whole slabs of pork spareribs into St. Louis–style ribs takes more prep time and effort than prepping whole spares or baby backs, but you can buy them from a store or butcher already cut. We (and other ribmasters) prefer to buy full spareribs and trim them ourselves so we can add the trimmings to our grill or smoker and snack on them (since they're done sooner than the rest of the ribs) or chop them up and add them to beans, dips, or other side dishes.

A WHOLE UNTRIMMED SPARERIB SLAB LOOKS LIKE THIS:

IT INCLUDES:

- the rib tips (the top portion of the slab)

- the breastbone (the top right corner)

- the skirt (the flap of meat on the bone side—see Chapter 1, page 5)

- the membrane (a thin, tough tissue lying against the rib bones)

A TRIMMED SPARERIB SLAB LOOKS LIKE THIS:

RIB TIPS

BREASTBONE

ST. LOUIS–STYLE SLAB

TRIMMED SKIRT

TRIMMING SPARERIBS TO MAKE ST. LOUIS–STYLE RIBS

Trimming your spareribs will give them the look of contest champions or slabs from finer rib joints.

Start with your slab meat side down on a cutting board. With a sharp butcher knife, start at the top of the second or third rib from the right (where the slab begins to taper down) and cut the rib tips across to the left, parallel with the bottom of the slab. Go back to the part on the right where the slab tapers down (the breastbone) and finish cutting off the rib tips at an angle as close to the breastbone as possible. This is the thickest part of the slab, and it has a lot of bone and cartilage, but when cooked it will yield delicious meat morsels, so we suggest you don't discard it.

The skirt is a flap of meat on the bony side of the ribs. Skirts vary from narrow to wide, depending on how much was left when the animal was butchered, and usually they have a piece of the diaphragm attached to them. Place a sharp knife against the bones beneath the skirt and slice it off in one piece parallel to the bones. Strip off the diaphragm and membrane (see Skinning Your Slab and Removing Excess Fat, below) and discard them, but save the meat.

Remove any excess fat, bone, gristle, or membrane from the rib tips and skirt meat, season them, if you like, and throw them on your cooker. They are just as tasty as the ribs, and they will be ready to eat in a little more than an hour while your ribs continue to cook. You can snack on them or, if you have the willpower, save some for chopping and adding to beans, dips, and other sides. If you don't want to cook the trimmings immediately, you can freeze them for future use.

SKINNING YOUR SLAB AND REMOVING EXCESS FAT

The final preparation step for St. Louis–style ribs is removing the membrane and any excess fat. This is done the same way for all types of ribs, so you'll find more information in Chapter 1, page 6.

HOOKED ON BLUE-RIBBON RIBS!

by Mike Lake, PhB, competition cooker and livestock expert

Our second time out in competitive cooking, we were in the Illinois State Championships (West Chicago, with Jim Burns), cooking on a homemade cooker built from a stainless-steel bulk milk tank. We won first in ribs and second in loin (back when you could cook it in a competition). Our team of four went to the bar afterward and spent more than our winnings celebrating the win—but it was great fun. I don't even want to tell you about the marinades that we used back then. We thought we were on top of it—that is, until we got to the next competition and got our butts kicked. Still loved it, though—I was hooked.

First-Time Grilled Baby Back Ribs

Serves 4 to 6

This is a good starter recipe for one of the most popular kinds of ribs. A few simple seasonings and a hot grill are all you need.

RUB

3 tablespoons seasoned salt

1 tablespoon paprika

2 teaspoons granulated onion

1 teaspoon granulated garlic

1 teaspoon finely ground black pepper

½ teaspoon cayenne

½ teaspoon ground celery seeds

RIBS

2 slabs baby back ribs

1 cup tomato-based barbecue sauce

Apple juice, for spraying (see page 13)

Combine all the ingredients for the rub in a small bowl and blend well. Season the ribs all over with the rub. Wrap the ribs tightly in plastic wrap and refrigerate overnight.

Remove the ribs from the refrigerator. Heat a cooker to medium to medium-high.

Oil the grate and place the unwrapped ribs on it bone side down over direct heat. Cover and cook for 45 minutes to 1 hour or until pull-apart tender, turning every 5 to 7 minutes and checking for flare-ups.

Move the ribs over indirect heat. Glaze the ribs with barbecue sauce on the bone side, then turn and glaze on the meat side. Cook the ribs bone side down for 7 to 10 minutes. Glaze on the meat side again and cook bone side down for another 7 to 10 minutes. You can apply sauce more than twice, if you like really sticky ribs, but keep the fire low to avoid caramelized ribs.

Transfer the ribs to a cutting board and let them rest, covered loosely with aluminum foil, for 10 to 15 minutes. Cut the ribs into individual pieces and serve.

Mama's Got the Blues Smoked and Grilled Baby Back Ribs

Serves 4 to 6

We're forever in awe of the many passionate female blues singers of the past and present who can belt out their pain like a mellowed-out cat on a hot tin roof—Bessie Smith, Ma Rainey, Janis Joplin, Nina Simone, Ida McBeth, Monique Danielle, to name a few. Mama's ribs are smoked first, then grilled over direct heat for glazing. And because sometimes Mama needs a drink, we've put one in the glaze.

2 slabs baby back ribs

RUB

2 teaspoons dried light brown sugar (see page 11)

2 teaspoons paprika

2 teaspoons seasoned salt

1 teaspoon finely ground black pepper

½ teaspoon dry mustard

½ teaspoon granulated garlic

¼ teaspoon ground celery seeds

MOP

1½ cups apple cider

¼ cup apple cider vinegar

¼ cup soy sauce

SAUCE

½ cup ketchup

2 tablespoons Worcestershire sauce

2 tablespoons bourbon, whiskey, rum, or apple cider

2 tablespoons unsalted butter

2 tablespoons light brown sugar

1 teaspoon celery seeds

Remove the ribs from the refrigerator. Heat a cooker to 250° to 275°F.

Combine all the ingredients for the rub in a small bowl and blend well. Season the ribs all over with the rub.

Oil the grate and place the ribs on it bone side down over indirect heat. Cover and cook for 45 minutes to 1 hour.

Meanwhile, stir together all the ingredients for the mop in a small bowl and set aside.

Combine all the ingredients for the sauce in a medium saucepan over medium heat. When the butter and brown sugar have melted, whisk to blend. Set aside.

Mop the meat side of the ribs with mop, turn, and mop the bone side. Cover and cook for 45 minutes to 1½ hours, or until pull-apart tender, turning and mopping the ribs 2 or 3 more times.

Glaze the ribs on both sides with the sauce, then move them over direct heat, bone side down. Grill for 5 to 7 minutes, or until the glaze browns and bubbles, then repeat the process on the meat side, watching carefully to make sure the ribs don't caramelize.

Transfer the ribs to a cutting board and let them rest, covered loosely with aluminum foil, for 10 to 15 minutes. Cut the ribs into individual pieces and serve with the remaining sauce.

Spotted Cow Smoked Baby Back Ribs

Serves 4 to 6

A cow with pig ribs? The cow in this instance symbolizes America's ever-growing multitude of micro and small breweries—from New Glarus, Wisconsin—home of Spotted Cow and other great brews, to Boulevard in Kansas City, Missouri; Empyrean in Lincoln, Nebraska; Harpoon in Windsor, Vermont; Peace Tree in Knoxville, Iowa; and hundreds more. The beer in this recipe marries so well with sugar, soy sauce, barbecue sauce, and garlic that beer drinkers and non-beer-drinkers will like the subtle and delicious accent it adds.

MARINADE

1 (12-ounce) bottle or can beer (anything but light)

½ cup soy sauce

½ cup tomato-based barbecue sauce

¼ cup clover or other mild-flavored honey

¾ cup firmly packed light brown sugar

1 teaspoon granulated garlic

RIBS

2 slabs baby back ribs

Combine all the ingredients for the marinade in a medium noncorrosive saucepan. Simmer over medium heat for about 5 minutes until the brown sugar is dissolved, whisking well. Set aside to cool. Reserve ½ cup for basting.

Place each slab of ribs in a 2-gallon resealable plastic bag. Divide the remaining marinade between the bags, seal tightly, and turn gently to completely coat the ribs. Refrigerate for 3 hours or preferably overnight, turning the bags occasionally.

Remove the ribs from the refrigerator and discard the marinade. Heat a cooker to 250° to 275°F.

Oil the grate and place the ribs on it bone side down over indirect heat. Cover and cook for 1 to 1½ hours. Turn and cook for another 1 to 1½ hours. Turn again and baste with the reserved marinade, then cook for another 30 to 45 minutes or until pull-apart tender.

Transfer the ribs to a cutting board and let them rest, covered loosely with aluminum foil, for 10 to 15 minutes. Cut the ribs into individual pieces and serve.

Sassy Smoked Hot Pepper-Glazed Baby Back Ribs

Serves 6 to 8

These ribs will put some tingle on your lips and a smile on your face. Even if you're wary of foods containing hot peppers and hot sauce, be bold and take a bite of these ribs. You may be surprised to find that the sweet and fiery combination is to your liking. If they are too mild for you, add more jalapeños and hot sauce to the glaze. We prefer Louisiana hot sauce or Texas Pete, but you can use Tabasco, if that's what you have on hand.

3 slabs baby back ribs

Salt and freshly ground black pepper

SAUCE

2 cups apple cider

⅓ cup minced red onion

1 tablespoon minced jalapeño chile

½ cup ketchup

¼ cup tomato paste

2 tablespoons red wine vinegar

2 to 3 tablespoons firmly packed light brown sugar

2 tablespoons Louisiana hot sauce

2 teaspoons dry mustard

1 teaspoon ground coriander

1 teaspoon finely ground black pepper

Heat a cooker to 250° to 275°F. Remove the ribs from the refrigerator and season them all over with salt and pepper.

Oil the grate and place the ribs on it bone side down over indirect heat. Cover and cook for 1 to 1½ hours. Turn and cook for another 1 to 1½ hours.

Meanwhile, make the sauce by combining the cider, onion, and jalapeño in a medium saucepan. Bring to a boil over medium-high heat, then reduce the heat and simmer gently, uncovered, for 15 minutes or until reduced to 1 cup. Add the ketchup, tomato paste, vinegar, brown sugar to taste, cayenne, and pepper, stir until the sugar dissolves, then remove from the heat. Set aside.

Turn the ribs and cook for another 30 to 45 minutes or until pull-apart tender, glazing the ribs with sauce at 10-minute intervals during the last 30 minutes of cooking.

Transfer the ribs to a cutting board and let them rest, covered loosely with aluminum foil, for 10 to 15 minutes. Cut the ribs into individual pieces and serve with the remaining glaze.

THE GREAT CLEVELAND RIB MASSACRE

by John Raven, PhB, Commissioner of Barbecue

Did I ever tell you about the time Cuzin Homer Page and I went to Cleveland, Ohio, to participate in the Great American Rib Cook-Off?

It all started in 1973, when I drafted Homer to be part of my Super Chili team. Homer was a great people person, and everyone enjoyed being around him. He did several cook-offs with me and then decided to strike out on his own. Homer was not a chili cook. He never made chili good enough for the hogs to eat, except for the one time he beat me at a local cook-off.

When I started judging barbecue at the Taylor International Barbecue cook-off, Homer tagged along. The next year, he took the family smoker, entered the competition, smoked a turkey, and won something. He decided he was a barbecue cook.

He made a couple of homemade barrel cookers and started winning right off the bat. He was good. He seldom went to a cook-off where he did not win something.

Homer and I were best friends and hung out together a lot. He built a barbecue joint on wheels and went into business in Temple, Texas. He sold out the first day and was in the business, with the best barbecue in that part of the country.

Somewhere along the line I put Homer in contact with one of the big-time barbecuers—I think it was Billy Bones Wall out of Michigan. Billy Bones told Homer about the commercial cook-offs, where tons of money could be made, and Homer decided to give it a try.

We required a few things like a barbecue trailer for a setup. Homer had the "Special Events" trailer built. I built the cabinets and counters for the trailer. It was flat nice. There was a lot of work involved in getting all this stuff done, and we did it.

The next thing was neither of us had ever cooked any ribs. We had to learn how.

On a very hot August afternoon, Homer, his son Todd, and I crawled in Homer's old pickup with trailer attached and headed for Cleveland, Ohio. We left Tuesday, and about sundown Wednesday we arrived in Cleveland. The only problem on the way was an

1985 NATIONAL RIB COOK·OFF

AC compressor failure at Columbus, Ohio. We just cut the belt and kept on trucking.

We found the cook site in downtown Cleveland and dollied down the trailer, then found our hotel and checked in. Bright and early Thursday morning we were on the cook-off site and set about getting the show ready. We also had to go find a hardware store and a grocery store for things we had not brought. It was a full day. That night the rest of the crew arrived: Homer's wife, his two daughters, his stepdaughter, Perry, and Smitty.

Friday was the first day of the cook-off. I was in charge of the grills. We had three three-foot by sixteen-foot grills. We started with two, which proved to be enough.

We had come up with the deal of par-boiling the ribs in seasoned water. When they were done, they came to me and my two hired hands at the grills. We put them on bone side down and mopped them with Homer's house sauce. Later we turned the slabs and glazed the meat side. They were really good.

The whole deal is sort of hazy in my memory now, as we worked three days from seven in the morning until two the next morning. Talk about being tired! Homer didn't get rich, but we did make enough money to pay for the trip. My cut was ten days of "vacation."

The thing I remember most about the trip was it killed my taste for ribs. For three days most of what I ate was ribs. Since then I have had little appetite for them.

Guilin Smoked Baby Back Ribs

Serves 4 to 6

One of our favorite cuisines besides barbecue is Chinese food, and we love this recipe for Chinese-style ribs. Guilin, China, is famous for its outstanding natural beauty, and a boat trip down its Li River will make you feel like you've gone back to the time when dinosaurs roamed the earth. Guilin's delicious famous chili sauce gets its distinct flavor from a mixture of chili, garlic, and fermented soybeans, but you can substitute Sriracha chili sauce, if that's what you have on hand.

MARINADE

1 cup hoisin sauce

½ cup plum sauce

⅓ cup oyster sauce

¼ cup sake

¼ cup clover or other mild-flavored honey

2 tablespoons soy sauce

2 tablespoons red wine vinegar

1 tablespoon dark sesame oil

1 tablespoon Guilin or Sriracha chili sauce

½ teaspoon five-spice powder

1 tablespoon freshly grated orange zest

10 garlic cloves, pressed

¼ cup peeled, grated fresh ginger

¼ cup finely minced scallion, both green and white parts

RIBS

2 slabs baby back ribs

Combine all the ingredients for the marinade in a small bowl and mix well. Place each slab of ribs in a 2-gallon resealable plastic bag. Divide the marinade between the bags, seal tightly, and turn to gently and completely coat the ribs. Refrigerate for at least 2 hours and up to overnight for more flavor, turning the bags occasionally.

Remove the ribs from the refrigerator and reserve the marinade. Heat a cooker to 250° to 275°F.

Transfer the reserved marinade to a small saucepan and bring it to a boil over high heat. Reduce the heat and simmer for 2 to 3 minutes. Set aside.

Oil the grate and place the ribs on it bone side down over indirect heat. Cover and cook for 1 to 1½ hours. Turn and cook for another 1 to 1½ hours. Turn and baste with the boiled marinade and cook for another 30 to 45 minutes, or until pull-apart tender, basting occasionally but stopping 15 minutes before removing the ribs from the cooker.

Transfer the ribs to a cutting board and let them rest, covered loosely with aluminum foil, for 10 to 15 minutes. While the ribs rest, boil any remaining marinade for 1 to 2 minutes. Cut the ribs into individual pieces and serve with the marinade.

Memphis-Style Grilled Baby Back Ribs

Serves 4 to 6

Memphis, known as the Pork Barbecue Capital of the Universe, is a great place to have ribs. We have been known to call it Rib City! Can you get these ribs at Payne's or A&R or the Bar-B-Q Shop? They are some of our favorite places, but you won't find these exact ribs there. Citizens in Rib City might argue about whether this recipe is Memphis style, but taste these ribs and you'll say, "I love Memphis!"

2 slabs baby back ribs

2 teaspoons salt

2 teaspoons coarsely ground black pepper

MOP

1 cup red wine vinegar

2 cups finely diced yellow onion

2 cloves garlic, pressed

¼ cup prepared yellow mustard

½ cup firmly packed light brown sugar

½ teaspoon Louisiana hot sauce

2 cups ketchup

2 lemons, thinly sliced

Remove the ribs from the refrigerator and sprinkle them with the salt and pepper. Heat a cooker to medium to medium-high.

To make the mop, place the vinegar, onion, garlic, mustard, brown sugar, and hot sauce in a blender and blend until smooth. Pour the pureed mixture into a medium saucepan over medium heat, add the ketchup, and simmer, uncovered, for 20 minutes, stirring occasionally. Add the lemon slices and simmer for 5 more minutes, stirring occasionally. If you'd like, reserve some for serving. Remove and discard the lemon and set aside both portions.

Oil the grate and place the ribs on it bone side down over direct heat. Grill for 45 minutes to 1 hour, or until pull-apart tender, turning every 7 to 10 minutes and brushing with the mop.

Transfer the ribs to a cutting board and let them rest, covered loosely with aluminum foil, for 10 to 15 minutes. Cut the ribs into individual pieces and serve with the reserved mopping sauce, if desired.

Sedona Sunset Smoked Baby Back Ribs

Serves 4 to 6

After a busy day exploring the countryside on foot or by car, come home to these easy-to-fix ribs, which remind us of a late-afternoon gathering of friends at a Sedona cookout with scenic red cliffs in the background. When you can't be in Sedona, you can call forth familiar Arizona flavors with these ribs.

RUB

1 teaspoon dried light brown sugar (see page 11)

1 teaspoon chili powder

1 teaspoon garlic powder

1 teaspoon onion powder

1 teaspoon paprika

½ teaspoon ground thyme

¼ teaspoon crushed dried rosemary

¼ teaspoon salt

¼ teaspoon freshly ground black pepper

RIBS

2 slabs baby back ribs

SAUCE

½ cup chili sauce

¼ cup honey

1 tablespoon apple cider vinegar

1 teaspoon granulated onion

1½ teaspoons Dijon mustard

1½ teaspoons Worcestershire sauce

Combine all the ingredients for the rub in a small bowl and blend. Season the ribs all over with the rub, wrap tightly in plastic wrap, and refrigerate for at least 2 hours and up to overnight.

Remove the ribs from the refrigerator. Heat a cooker to 250° to 275°F.

Oil the grate and place the unwrapped ribs on it bone side down over indirect heat. Cover and cook for 1 to 1½ hours. Turn and cook for another 1 to 1½ hours.

Meanwhile, combine all the sauce ingredients in a small bowl and mix well. Set aside.

Turn the ribs and cook for another 30 to 45 minutes, or until pull-apart tender, glazing the ribs with the sauce at 10-minute intervals during the last 30 minutes of cooking.

Transfer the ribs to a cutting board and let them rest, covered loosely with aluminum foil, for 10 to 15 minutes. While the ribs rest, boil the remaining sauce for 1 to 2 minutes, if desired. Cut the ribs into individual pieces and serve with the sauce.

New England Maple-Brined Smoked Pork Rib Roast

Serves 8 to 10

These ribs aren't eligible for the rib category in barbecue contests, but technically they are ribs—the meatiest ribs you'll ever serve. Use real maple syrup, not maple-flavored syrup. We're big fans of maple syrup from Vermont, New Hampshire, and Maine. Using so much of the precious stuff in brine is a big sacrifice, but when you taste the results we believe you'll say it's worth it.

BRINE

6 cups water

¼ cup firmly packed light brown sugar

½ cup kosher salt

½ cup plus ¼ cup grade B maple syrup

¼ cup malt vinegar

2 teaspoons vanilla extract

3 cups ice cubes

PORK

1 (8-rib) pork loin roast (about 5 pounds)

RUB

1 tablespoon crushed dried rosemary

1 tablespoon coarsely ground black pepper

1 tablespoon dried minced garlic

1 tablespoon kosher salt

To make the brine, combine the water, brown sugar, salt, ½ cup of the maple syrup, the vinegar, and the vanilla in a 2-gallon resealable plastic bag; stir until completely dissolved. Stir in the ice cubes. (This quickly lowers the temperature of the brine so it doesn't begin to cook the meat.) Place the pork in the bag and seal it tightly. Place the bag in a large pan and refrigerate for 24 hours.

Remove the pork from the brine and discard the brine. Rinse the pork with cold water and pat dry with paper towels. At this point, the pork can be wrapped tightly in plastic wrap and refrigerated for up to 1 day.

Remove the rib roast from the refrigerator. Heat a cooker to 250° to 275°F.

Combine all the ingredients for the rub in a small bowl and blend well. Sprinkle over the rib roast. Oil the grate and place the roast on it, rib side down. Cook for 1 to 1½ hours, or until it reaches at least 140°F or the desired temperature on a meat thermometer. Remove from the cooker and cover loosely with foil. Increase the cooker temperature to 300° to 350°F.

Glaze the pork with the remaining ¼ cup of maple syrup and cook for 7 to 10 minutes.

Transfer the pork to a cutting board and let it rest, covered loosely with aluminum foil, for 15 to 20 minutes. Carve between the rib bones so each person receives a thick rib chop.

Smoked Bourbon-Glazed Baby Back Ribs

Serves 4 to 6

Bourbon is enjoying renewed popularity in barbecuing these days. It really complements and brings out the flavor of smoked pork. We've heard that Jim Beam is the best-selling brand of bourbon out of Kentucky. We recommend it for this recipe, but if you're partial to another brand, use it instead.

2 slabs baby back ribs

Salt and freshly ground pepper

Apple juice, for spraying (see page 13)

SAUCE

5 tablespoons clover or other
   mild-flavored honey

¼ cup Jim Beam Kentucky bourbon
   or your favorite brand

2 tablespoons hoisin sauce

1 tablespoon Dijon mustard

1 tablespoon plum sauce

2 teaspoons molasses

2 teaspoons soy sauce

2 teaspoons Worcestershire sauce

1 teaspoon peeled, grated fresh ginger

1 teaspoon hot chili paste

¼ teaspoon salt

¼ teaspoon freshly ground black pepper

1 cup pineapple juice

Heat a cooker to 250° to 275°F. Season the ribs all over with the salt and pepper.

Oil the grate and place the ribs on it bone side down over indirect heat. Cover and cook for 1 to 1½ hours. Turn and spray with apple juice, then cook for another 1 to 1½ hours, occasionally turning and spraying with apple juice.

Meanwhile, combine all the ingredients for the sauce in a small saucepan over medium-high heat. Bring to a boil, then reduce the heat and simmer for 15 minutes, stirring often. Set aside.

Turn the ribs and cook for 30 to 45 minutes more, or until pull-apart tender, glazing the ribs with the sauce at 10-minute intervals during the last 30 minutes of cooking.

Transfer the ribs to a cutting board and let them rest, covered loosely with aluminum foil, for 10 to 15 minutes. Cut the ribs into individual pieces and serve.

Mr. Piggy's Revenge Grilled Chipotle Baby Back Ribs

Serves 4 to 6

When you want ribs with attitude, these are it! If you're using this glaze in a barbecue competition, make sure you put the marmalade and chipotles in a blender and puree them so you don't have any large pieces of orange peel to get you disqualified.

RUB

¼ cup white cane sugar

2 tablespoons seasoned salt

1 tablespoon onion salt

2 teaspoons garlic salt

1 teaspoon celery salt

2 tablespoons paprika

1 tablespoons chili powder

2 teaspoons lemon pepper

1 teaspoon freshly ground black pepper

½ teaspoon ground ginger

½ teaspoon dry mustard

½ teaspoon ground chipotle chile

RIBS

2 slabs baby back ribs

SAUCE

½ cup tomato-based barbecue sauce

1½ tablespoons orange marmalade

1½ tablespoons chopped chipotle chiles in adobo sauce

¼ cup water

Heat a cooker to medium to medium-high.

Combine all the ingredients for the rub in a small bowl and blend well. Season the ribs all over with the rub.

Combine all the ingredients for the sauce in a small bowl and set aside.

Oil the grate and place the ribs on it bone side down over direct heat. Cover and cook for 45 minutes to 1 hour, or until pull-apart tender, turning every 5 to 7 minutes and glazing with the sauce during the last 30 minutes of cooking.

Transfer the ribs to a cutting board and let them rest, covered loosely with aluminum foil, for 10 to 15 minutes. While the ribs are resting, boil the remaining sauce for 1 to 2 minutes, if desired, before serving with the ribs.

Spicy Grilled Baby Back Ribs

Serves 4 to 6

Some people use dry rubs, some use wet marinades, and some swear by a hybrid—a wet paste. Years ago, when Chef Paul was teaching cooking classes in South Korea, he just couldn't find barbecue spices. Luckily, his wife had brought some spices to use in their kitchen, so he raided those and made a paste.

PASTE

¼ cup firmly packed light brown sugar

2 tablespoons ground cumin

1 tablespoon chili powder

1 tablespoon hot smoked paprika

1 tablespoon crushed dried thyme

2 teaspoons celery seeds

1 teaspoon cayenne

1 teaspoon Chinese five-spice powder

¼ teaspoon ground cloves

Salt and freshly ground black pepper

1½ cups strong brewed coffee

2 tablespoons Sriracha sauce

2 tablespoons molasses

1 tablespoon Worcestershire sauce

7 to 8 large cloves garlic, pressed

1 tablespoon peeled, minced fresh ginger

4 beef bouillon cubes

RIBS

2 slabs pork baby back racks ribs

Barbecue sauce, for serving

To make the paste, combine the brown sugar, cumin, chili powder, paprika, thyme, celery seed, cayenne, five-spice powder, cloves, and some salt and black pepper in a small bowl and blend well. In a medium saucepan, combine the coffee, Sriracha sauce, molasses, Worcestershire sauce, garlic, ginger, and bouillon cubes. Cook over medium-low heat, stirring often, until the bouillon cubes dissolve. Sprinkle the dry mixture into the liquid mixture, stirring constantly, and mix until thoroughly combined. Remove from the heat and set aside to cool.

Rub the cooled paste all over the ribs, wrap tightly with plastic wrap, and refrigerate for at least 4 hours and up to overnight.

Remove the ribs from the refrigerator. Heat a cooker to medium to medium-high.

Oil the grate and place the unwrapped ribs on it bone side down over direct heat. Cover and cook for 45 minutes to 1 hour, or until pull-apart tender, turning every 5 to 7 minutes.

Transfer the ribs to a cutting board and let them rest, covered with aluminum foil, for 10 to 15 minutes. Cut into individual pieces and serve with barbecue sauce.

Smoked Garlic Cajun Baby Back Ribs

Serves 4 to 6

Don't be deterred by the details. Chef Paul has adapted this classic recipe as another easy starting place for beginners. You'll have more Cajun seasoning than you need, but you may even want to make a larger batch and store some of it in a cool, dry place for 2 or 3 months. It's great on all kinds of meat.

CAJUN SEASONING

4½ teaspoons ground white pepper

4½ teaspoon freshly ground black pepper

1 tablespoon ground red pepper
  (or cayenne for more heat)

1 tablespoon crushed dried thyme

1 tablespoon onion powder

1 tablespoon garlic powder

1½ teaspoons salt

PASTE

4 to 6 large cloves garlic, pressed

¼ cup seasoned salt

¼ cup prepared yellow mustard

2 tablespoons fresh lemon juice

RIBS

2 slabs baby back ribs

Apple juice, for spraying (see page 13)

SAUCE

1 (18-ounce) bottle tomato-
  based barbecue sauce

2 large cloves garlic, pressed

2 tablespoons seasoned salt

⅓ cup Worcestershire sauce

Combine all the ingredients for the Cajun seasoning in a small bowl and blend well. Set aside 2 tablespoons and ¼ cup and store the rest in a tightly sealed container in a cool, dark place for future use.

To make the paste, combine the garlic, 2 tablespoons Cajun seasoning, seasoned salt, yellow mustard, and lemon juice in a small bowl and blend. Slather the ribs all over with the paste, then wrap tightly in plastic wrap and refrigerate overnight.

Remove the ribs from the refrigerator. Heat a cooker to 250° to 275°F.

Oil the grate and place the unwrapped ribs on it bone side down over indirect heat. Cover and smoke for 1 to 1½ hours. Turn and spray with apple juice, then cook for another 1 to 1½ hours.

Meanwhile, make the sauce by combining the barbecue sauce, garlic, ¼ cup Cajun seasoning, seasoned salt, and Worcestershire sauce in a medium bowl and mix well.

Turn the ribs and cook for another 30 to 45 minutes, or until pull-apart tender, glazing the ribs with the sauce at 10-minute intervals during the last 30 minutes of cooking.

Transfer the ribs to a cutting board and let them rest, covered loosely with aluminum foil, for 10 to 15 minutes. Cut the ribs into individual pieces and serve.

Sugar-and-Spice Smoked Baby Back Ribs

Serves 4 to 6

These ribs are one of Ardie's favorites. He usually fixes them for artist friends of his wife, Gretchen, and him, who come to Kansas City for art fairs every spring and fall.

RUB

⅓ cup white cane sugar

1 tablespoon Lawry's Seasoned Salt

1 tablespoon hickory-flavored salt

2 teaspoons garlic salt

1 teaspoon onion salt

½ teaspoon celery salt

2 tablespoons paprika

2 teaspoons chili powder

2 teaspoons freshly ground black pepper

½ teaspoon ground cumin

¼ teaspoon ground cinnamon

1/8 teaspoon ground rosemary

¼ teaspoon cayenne

RIBS

2 slabs baby back ribs

Apple juice, for spraying (see page 13)

Barbecue sauce, for glazing and serving

Combine all the ingredients for the rub in a small bowl. Set aside ¼ cup of the rub and store the remainder in a tightly sealed container in a cool, dark place for 2 or 3 months for future use.

Season the ribs all over with the ¼ cup of rub. Wrap tightly in plastic wrap and refrigerate for at least 8 and up to 24 hours.

Remove the ribs from the refrigerator. Heat a cooker to to 250° to 275°F.

Oil the grate and place the unwrapped ribs on it bone side down over indirect heat. Cover and cook for 1 to 1½ hours. Turn and spray the ribs with apple juice, then cook for another 1 to 1½ hours. Turn and spray again, then cook for another 30 to 45 minutes, or until pull-apart tender, glazing the ribs with barbecue sauce at 10-minute intervals during the last 30 minutes of cooking.

Transfer the ribs to a cutting board and let them rest, covered loosely with aluminum foil, for 10 to 15 minutes. While the ribs are resting, boil the remaining sauce for 1 to 2 minutes, if desired. Cut the ribs into individual pieces and serve with the sauce.

& Every-thing Nice

Southern-Flavor-Mouth Grilled Baby Back Ribs

Serves 4 to 6

We've seen many versions of southern grilled ribs. Chef Paul has adapted this one. It's got more tomato flavor than vinegar, so they might not favor it in the Carolinas, but other southerners would sure like it.

2 slabs baby back ribs

MARINADE

⅔ cup water

½ cup red wine vinegar

2 teaspoons sea salt

1 teaspoon finely ground black pepper

SAUCE

2 cups ketchup

1 cup water

½ cup apple cider vinegar

⅓ cup Worcestershire sauce

¼ cup prepared yellow mustard

4 tablespoons (½ stick) unsalted butter

½ cup firmly packed light brown sugar

1 teaspoon Louisiana hot sauce

1 teaspoon salt

1 teaspoon freshly ground black pepper

Place each slab of ribs in a 2-gallon resealable plastic bag.

Combine all the ingredients for the marinade in a small bowl and stir. Divide the marinade between the bags, seal tightly, and turn gently to completely coat the ribs. Refrigerate for at least 3 hours and up to overnight, turning occasionally.

Remove the ribs from the refrigerator. Heat a cooker to medium to medium-high.

Combine all the sauce ingredients in a medium saucepan and bring to a boil. Reduce the heat to low, cover, and simmer for 30 minutes. Set aside to cool.

Remove the ribs from the marinade and transfer the marinade to a medium saucepan. Bring it to a boil over high heat. Reduce the heat and simmer for 2 to 3 minutes. Set aside.

Oil the grate and place the ribs on it bone side down over direct heat. Cover and cook for 45 minutes to 1 hour, or until pull-apart tender, turning every 5 to 7 minutes and basting with the reserved marinade. Glaze with the sauce and grill for 8 to 10 minutes more. Turn, glaze again, if desired, and grill for 8 to 10 minutes more.

Transfer the ribs to a cutting board and let them rest, covered loosely with aluminum foil, for 10 to 15 minutes. Cut the ribs into individual pieces and serve.

Aunt Mae's Grilled Country-Style Ribs

Serves 4 to 6

Ardie's aunt Mae was sharp-witted, loving, and the epitome of candor. Her lively personality added a lot of sparkle to the Missouri Ozarks, where she lived her entire life. These tender, flavorful ribs will be ready to serve in just over an hour—easy, basic, and always a hit.

4 pounds country-style ribs

2 tablespoons garlic salt

2 teaspoons freshly ground black pepper

SAUCE

1¼ cups ketchup

¾ cup firmly packed light brown sugar

½ cup chili sauce

2 tablespoons apple cider vinegar

2 teaspoons liquid smoke

1 teaspoon ground coriander

1 teaspoon granulated garlic

1 teaspoon ground allspice

½ teaspoon cayenne

Heat a cooker to medium to medium-high. Season the ribs all over with garlic salt and pepper and set aside for 1 hour.

Combine all the ingredients for the sauce in a medium saucepan over medium heat. Simmer for 10 minutes, stirring occasionally. Set aside.

Oil the grate and place the ribs on it over direct heat. Cover and cook for 35 to 45 minutes, or until tender (or they read 140°F or higher, if desired, on a meat thermometer), turning and glazing with the sauce every 7 to 10 minutes.

Transfer the ribs to a serving platter and let them rest, covered loosely with aluminum foil, for 10 to 15 minutes. While the ribs are resting, boil the remaining sauce for 1 to 2 minutes before serving with the ribs.

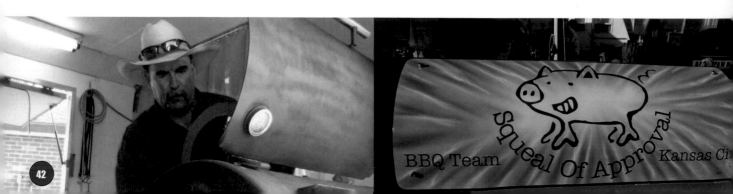

Smoked Orange-Glazed Country-Style Ribs

Serves 4 to 6

This gives you the ideal makings for a citrusy Florida-style rib sandwich with no bones. Put the ribs on a slice of white sandwich bread, splash some of your favorite barbecue sauce on the meat, top it with another slice of bread, and enjoy!

RUB

2 tablespoons lemon pepper

1 teaspoon granulated garlic

½ teaspoon ground allspice

¼ teaspoon cayenne

RIBS

4 pounds country-style ribs

SAUCE

1 cup water

1 (6-ounce) can tomato paste

½ cup firmly packed light brown sugar

¼ cup fresh orange juice

2 tablespoons white wine vinegar

1 tablespoon Dijon mustard

1 tablespoon Worcestershire sauce

½ teaspoon freshly ground black pepper

Heat a cooker to 250° to 275°F.

Combine all the ingredients for the rub in a small bowl and blend well. Season the ribs all over with the rub and set aside. You also can wrap them tightly in plastic wrap and refrigerate them up to overnight and remove them from the refrigerator 1 hour before cooking.

Combine all the ingredients for the sauce in a small saucepan over medium heat. Stir to combine and simmer for about 15 minutes. Set aside.

Oil the grate and place the unwrapped ribs on it over indirect heat. Cover and cook for 30 to 45 minutes. Turn and cook for another 30 to 45 minutes, or until tender (or they read 140°F or higher, if desired, on a meat thermometer), turning and glazing the ribs with the sauce every 10 minutes for the last 30 minutes of cooking. Watch carefully so the ribs don't caramelize or burn.

Transfer the ribs to a serving platter and let them rest, covered loosely with aluminum foil, for 10 to 15 minutes. While the ribs are resting, boil the remaining sauce for 1 to 2 minutes before serving with the ribs.

Rib Mountain Grilled Country-Style Ribs

Serves 4 to 6

It has been said that Rib Mountain, a.k.a. Rib Hill, is the burial place of America's most famous legendary giant, Paul Bunyan. Located in Marathon County, Wisconsin, near Wausau, the town and the mountain share the same name. There's even a Rib River nearby. It's our kind of place. And since rumor has it that the real Johnny Appleseed paid his respects to Paul Bunyan on Rib Mountain, the Baron prepared this special applesauce barbecue sauce to commemorate the occasion. These meaty country-style ribs with spicy seasonings embraced by applesauce pay tribute to two American legends, as well as your guests. Go ahead and serve apple pie à la mode for dessert!

SAUCE

2 cups applesauce

2 cups ketchup

2 tablespoons fresh lemon juice

2 tablespoons Worcestershire sauce

2 teaspoons prepared yellow mustard

1 teaspoon granulated onion

1 teaspoon granulated garlic

½ teaspoon ground celery seeds

½ teaspoon salt

½ teaspoon freshly ground black pepper

¼ teaspoon ground chipotle chile

RUB

2 tablespoons garlic salt

1 tablespoon lemon pepper

1 teaspoon white cane sugar

RIBS

4 pounds country-style ribs

Heat a cooker to medium to medium-high.

Combine all the ingredients for the sauce in a medium saucepan over medium heat and stir. Cover and simmer for 15 minutes, stirring occasionally. Set aside.

Combine all the ingredients for the rub in a small bowl and blend well. Season the ribs all over with the rub.

Oil the grate and place the ribs on it over direct heat. Cover and cook for 35 to 45 minutes, or until tender (or they read 140°F or higher, if desired, on a meat thermometer), turning every 7 to 10 minutes and glazing with the sauce during the last 30 minutes of cooking.

Transfer the ribs to a serving platter and let them rest, covered loosely with aluminum foil, for 10 to 15 minutes. While the ribs are resting, boil the remaining sauce for 1 to 2 minutes before serving with the ribs.

Grilled Cuban Glazed Country-Style Ribs

Serves 4 to 6

When you're hungry for or ready to try some easy country-style ribs with a Caribbean accent, this recipe from the Baron's archives will not disappoint. You can put this marinade together in a flash or—as Ardie sometimes does—go to the Hispanic section of your supermarket and try Goya Mojo Criollo, Mojo Chipotle, or Bitter Orange.

MARINADE

¼ cup canola oil

¼ cup fresh orange juice

¼ cup fresh lime juice

2 teaspoons granulated garlic

2 teaspoons granulated onion

2 teaspoons finely ground black pepper

1 teaspoon ground cumin

1 teaspoon salt

1 teaspoon ground ginger

1 teaspoon ground allspice

1 teaspoon chili powder

RIBS

4 pounds country-style ribs

Combine all the ingredients for the marinade in a 2-gallon resealable plastic bag. Add the ribs, seal the bag tightly, and turn gently to coat the ribs. Refrigerate for at least 2 hours or overnight, turning the bag occasionally.

Heat a cooker to medium to medium-high.

Remove the ribs from the marinade and transfer the marinade to a medium saucepan. Bring it to a boil over medium-high heat. Reduce the heat and simmer for 2 to 3 minutes. Set aside.

Oil the grate and place the ribs on it over direct heat. Cover and cook for 35 to 45 minutes, or until tender (or they read 140°F or higher, if desired, on a meat thermometer), turning and basting with the boiled marinade every 7 to 10 minutes.

Transfer the ribs to a serving platter and let them rest, covered loosely with aluminum foil, for 10 to 15 minutes before serving.

KC Rib Doctor's Grilled Country-Style Ribs

Serves 4 to 6

Guy Simpson, the KC Rib Doctor, is known far and wide for his blue-ribbon award-winning barbecue rub. Although we're big fans of his rub, we asked Guy to show us how he can cook outstanding ribs without a rub. He's done it with this recipe!

MARINADE

1 cup Dr Pepper (not diet)

¼ cup dark soy sauce

2 tablespoons fresh lime juice

2 tablespoons canola oil

2 large cloves garlic, pressed

1 teaspoon liquid smoke

RIBS

4 pounds country-style ribs

Combine all the ingredients for the marinade in a medium bowl and stir. Place the ribs in a 2-gallon resealable plastic bag and add the marinade. Seal the bag tightly and turn gently to coat the ribs. Refrigerate for 2 to 4 hours, turning every hour.

Remove the ribs from the refrigerator. Heat a cooker to medium to medium-high.

Remove the ribs from the marinade and transfer the marinade to a small saucepan. Bring it to a boil over medium-high heat. Reduce the heat and simmer for 2 to 3 minutes. Set aside to cool.

Oil the grate and place the ribs on it over direct heat. Cover and cook for 35 to 45 minutes, or until tender (or until they reach 140°F or higher, if desired, on a meat thermometer), turning and basting with the boiled marinade every 7 to 10 minutes.

Transfer the ribs to a serving platter and let them rest, covered loosely with aluminum foil, for 10 to 15 minutes before serving.

Grilled Ginger-Plum-Glazed Country-Style Ribs

Serves 4 to 6

When the magic of fire and smoke is paired with the sweet and zesty flavors in this sauce, you'll enjoy some remarkably tasty ribs!

SAUCE

1 cup plum jam

¼ cup chopped scallion, both green and white parts

¼ cup fresh lemon juice

2 tablespoons hoisin sauce

1 tablespoon triple sec or other orange liqueur

1 tablespoon peeled, grated fresh ginger

1 teaspoon dry mustard

½ teaspoon ground habanero chile

RIBS

3 to 4 pounds country-style ribs

Heat a cooker to medium to medium-high.

Combine all the ingredients for the sauce in a blender and puree until smooth. Transfer half to a serving dish and set aside both portions.

Oil the grate and place the ribs on it over direct heat. Cover and cook for 35 to 45 minutes, or until tender (or until they reach 140°F or higher, if desired, on a meat thermometer), turning and glazing with the sauce every 7 to 10 minutes.

Transfer the ribs to a serving platter and let them rest, covered loosely with aluminum foil, for 10 to 15 minutes. Warm the other half of the reserved sauce and serve it with the ribs.

Basic BBQ Tea

Smoked Alabama-Style Country-Style Ribs

Serves 4 to 6

We've known Don McLemore, Chris Lilly, and the whole Big Bob Gibson family for so long that thinking of Alabama barbecue calls to mind that classic white northern Alabama barbecue sauce that Big Bob Gibson's has made famous. On the other hand, Alabama barbecue also calls to mind one of our favorite tomato-based sauces at Bob Sykes Bar-B-Q in Bessemer. Truth is, you can find a variety of great sauces and barbecue throughout the state, so while we think most Alabamans would approve of these ribs, keep in mind that there are many other ways to flavor a rib in Alabama.

MARINADE

8 cups apple cider vinegar

6 tablespoons salt

1 tablespoon cayenne

1½ tablespoons crushed red pepper

¼ cup molasses, or ½ cup firmly packed light brown sugar

RIBS

4 pounds country-style ribs

Combine all the ingredients for the marinade in a small bowl and stir. Reserve and refrigerate half the marinade. Pour the remaining marinade into a 2-gallon resealable plastic bag, add the ribs, seal the bag tightly, and turn gently a few times to completely coat the ribs. Refrigerate for at least 4 hours and up to overnight, turning the bag occasionally.

Remove the ribs from the refrigerator and reserve the marinade. Heat a cooker to 250° to 275°F.

Transfer the reserved marinade to a medium saucepan and bring it to a boil over medium-high heat. Reduce the heat and simmer for 2 to 3 minutes. Set aside.

Oil the grate and place the ribs on it over indirect heat. Cover and cook for 30 to 45 minutes. Turn and baste with the boiled marinade, then cook for 30 to 45 minutes more. Turn and baste again, then cook for about 30 minutes more, or until tender.

Transfer the ribs to a serving platter and let them rest, covered loosely with aluminum foil, for 10 to 15 minutes. While the ribs are resting, warm the reserved marinade, if desired, before serving with the ribs.

Link's Bayou Swamp Grilled Country-Style Ribs

Serves 4 to 6

No wonder (missing) Link goes to his hiding place in the bayou to eat these ribs. The gators are resting for their nocturnal feeding time, it's too hot for the mosquitoes, and everybody else will just have to wait. He'll treat friends and family to a feast of swamp ribs come Fat Tuesday, but today they are his alone to enjoy. There's a secret ingredient in Link's homemade sauce, but he won't tell us. Our friend Billy Rodgers thinks it could be Gator Hammock hot sauce. Knowing Link, we wonder if it's moonshine. For extra fire and accent, sprinkle the finished ribs with Louisiana hot sauce—red, green, or both.

RUB

4 teaspoons Hungarian paprika

2 teaspoons granulated onion

2 teaspoons granulated garlic

2 teaspoons cayenne

2 teaspoons crushed dried oregano

2 teaspoons crushed dried thyme

2 teaspoons freshly ground black pepper

1 teaspoon rubbed sage

1 teaspoon gumbo filé

1 teaspoon salt

RIBS

4 pounds country-style ribs

Apple juice, for spraying
   (see page 13)

Heat a cooker to medium to medium-high.

Combine all the ingredients for the rub in a small bowl and blend. Season the ribs all over with the rub and set them aside for 15 minutes.

Oil the grate and place the unwrapped ribs on it over direct heat. Cover and cook for 30 to 45 minutes, or until tender, turning and basting with apple juice every 7 to 10 minutes.

Transfer the ribs to a serving platter and let them rest, covered loosely with aluminum foil, for 10 to 15 minutes before serving.

Grilled Tennessee-Style Spareribs

Serves 6

How bone-in pork rib chops came to be associated with western Tennessee is just as much a mystery to us as to how baby back ribs came to be associated with Memphis. We'll leave it to social anthropologists or historians to figure that out.

You would not believe the comments we got when we decided to put this recipe in a rib book. Everyone said, "These are pork chops!" We admit it is a big stretch to call these spareribs, but technically they are rib chops. They're also very popular in Texas and in our Kansas City backyards, and we think you'll like them no matter where you call home.

6 (10-ounce) bone-in pork rib chops, 1 inch thick

Canola oil, for brushing

SAUCE

1 cup ketchup

3 tablespoons molasses

2 tablespoons prepared yellow mustard

2 tablespoons apple cider vinegar

1 tablespoon light brown sugar

1 tablespoon Worcestershire sauce

1 teaspoon hot sauce

1 teaspoon granulated garlic

½ teaspoon kosher salt

Freshly ground black pepper

½ cup water

RUB

2 teaspoons freshly ground black pepper

1½ teaspoons paprika

1½ teaspoons dried light brown sugar (see page 11)

1½ teaspoons kosher salt

1 teaspoon dry mustard

1 teaspoon granulated garlic

1 teaspoon granulated onion

Pinch of cayenne

Heat a cooker to medium-high. Let the pork chops sit at room temperature for at least 30 minutes before cooking.

Combine all the ingredients for the sauce in a medium saucepan over medium heat and stir. Bring to a boil, then reduce the heat and simmer for 10 minutes, or until slightly thickened, stirring occasionally. Set aside and reserve some for serving.

Combine all the ingredients for the rub in a small bowl and blend.

Lightly brush each chop on all sides with a bit of canola oil, then sprinkle liberally with the rub.

Oil the grate and place the chops on it over direct heat. Cover and cook for 7 to 10 minutes. Turn and cook for 7 to 10 minutes more, or until the chops are firm to the touch and register 140°F or higher, if desired, on a meat thermometer. Transfer the chops to the cool zone and glaze both sides with sauce. Cook for 10 minutes. Repeat as desired.

Transfer the ribs to a serving platter and let them rest, covered loosely with aluminum foil, for 10 to 15 minutes before serving with the reserved sauce.

THE WORST RIBS WE NEVER ATE!
Ribs We'd Like to Forget But Can't, Because They Were so Bad!

Like most rib aficionados, if we're served bad ribs, we'll never go back. Fortunately the good ribs have far exceeded the bad. But we do remember a few that were so bad we couldn't eat them.

There was a popular rib joint in a town in central Kansas. The pitmaster/proprietor had a statewide reputation for great barbecue. We had enjoyed his barbecue and enjoyed visiting with him each time our travels brought us through his town. Our final visit, however, was very disappointing. We ordered a slab of pork spares to go. He told us as he prepped our order, "You know, I've taken to liking cheese lately, more than I like barbecue." That remark, and the fact that we were the only customers and it was the dinner hour, should have given us a clue.

Later, when we unwrapped the slab, expecting to feast on the ribs he was known for, the letdown was sharp and immediate. What we got were tasteless boiled ribs sauced with watered-down, canned condensed tomato soup—nothing like the old days. One bite and the whole slab went in the nearest Dumpster.

Then there was a downtown café in a scenic little town in central Iowa. We stopped for lunch, and as luck would have it, the special of the day was "barbecued ribs." Ignoring Gretchen's warning (she's been through this routine with Ardie more than once), we ordered the special. The pork spareribs were boiled, not barbecued, and even at that, they were not tender. The sweet tomatoey barbecue sauce we used could not redeem the bland flavor of the meat. We got similar ribs in a barbecue joint, now closed, in Sarasota, Florida.

Wasted ribs are a darned shame, and so unnecessary!

Smoked Coffee-Rubbed Spareribs

Serves 4 to 6

Long before high-caffeine "energy drinks" became popular, ribmasters, especially in Texas, were putting strong coffee, ketchup, and Worcestershire sauce to good use with their BlackJack sauce. We've added some sugar and vinegar to the mix for a surefire wake-up call to your taste buds. This is coffee that sticks to your ribs!

RUB

2 tablespoons dried light brown sugar (see page 11)

2 tablespoons white cane sugar

2 tablespoons garlic salt

2 tablespoons onion salt

2 tablespoons paprika

1 tablespoon instant espresso coffee powder

1 tablespoon finely ground black pepper

1 teaspoon ground coriander

1 teaspoon crushed dried thyme

½ teaspoon cayenne

¼ teaspoon ground bay leaf

RIBS

2 slabs spareribs

Apple juice, for spraying (see page 13)

SAUCE

2 cups ketchup

1 cup strong brewed coffee

1 cup Worcestershire sauce

½ cup apple cider vinegar

½ cup firmly packed brown sugar

1 tablespoon mild chili powder

2 teaspoons granulated garlic

1 teaspoon granulated onion

1 teaspoon ground jalapeño chile powder

½ teaspoon celery seeds

1 teaspoon salt

1 teaspoon finely ground black pepper

Heat a cooker to 250° to 275°F.

Combine all the ingredients for the rub in a medium bowl and blend. Sprinkle all over the ribs and let sit for 1 hour. You also can refrigerate the ribs, tightly wrapped in plastic wrap, overnight, but remove them from the refrigerator about 1 hour before you cook them to bring them to room temperature.

Oil the grate and place the unwrapped ribs on it bone side down over indirect heat. Cover and cook for 1½ hours. Spray with apple juice, turn, and cook for about 1½ hours more before turning and basting with apple juice again.

Meanwhile, combine all the ingredients for the sauce in a medium saucepan over medium heat and stir. Simmer for 25 minutes, then set aside.

Cook the ribs for 1 to 1½ hours longer, then test to see if the ribs are pull-apart tender. When tender, cook for 30 minutes longer, glazing the ribs with sauce every 10 minutes or as often as desired.

Transfer the ribs to a cutting board and let them rest, covered loosely with aluminum foil, for 10 to 15 minutes. Cut the ribs into individual pieces and serve with the remaining sauce.

Grilled Whiskey Citrus Spareribs

Serves 4 to 6

Some folks prefer Kentucky bourbon in this recipe. We think Tennessee sour mash whiskey works best, but it's your choice. After the citrus brine does its magic, the whiskey glaze makes a mellow spicy finish. If you don't like a lot of spicy fire in your ribs, omit or reduce the pepper flakes. These ribs, trimmed St. Louis style and soaked in brine, are more meaty and forgiving than baby back ribs.

2 slabs spareribs

BRINE

1¼ cups fresh orange juice

½ cup fresh lemon juice

¼ cup fresh lime juice

½ cup water

3 tablespoons kosher salt

2 teaspoons crushed dried oregano

1 teaspoon crushed dried thyme

1 tablespoon crushed red pepper

SAUCE

1 cup Jack Daniel's Sour Mash Tennessee Whiskey

½ cup firmly packed light brown sugar

2 tablespoons unsalted butter

1 teaspoon kosher salt

½ teaspoon freshly ground black pepper

½ teaspoon crushed red pepper

If possible, place each slab in a 2-gallon resealable plastic bag. If your slabs are very large, you may need to cut each slab in half and place each half in a separate bag so you'll have enough room for the brine.

Combine all the ingredients for the brine in a medium bowl and stir until the salt is completely dissolved.

Add the brine to the plastic bags, seal tightly, and turn gently to completely coat the ribs. Refrigerate for 3 to 6 hours, but no longer.

Heat a cooker to medium to medium-high. Remove the ribs from the brine, rinse them in cold water, and pat dry.

Combine all the ingredients for the sauce in a medium saucepan over medium heat and stir until the butter is melted. Set aside.

Oil the grate and place the ribs on it bone side down over direct heat. Cover and cook for 2½ to 3½ hours, or until pull-apart tender, turning every 10 to 15 minutes and glazing with the sauce every 10 minutes during the last 30 minutes of cooking.

Transfer the ribs to a cutting board and let them rest, covered loosely with aluminum foil, for 10 to 15 minutes. While the ribs are resting, boil the remaining sauce for 1 to 2 minutes, if desired, before serving with the ribs.

Smoked Raspberry Glazed Spareribs

Serves 4 to 6

If you're a fan of sweet-and-sour chicken, you'll like these ribs, which give you similar flavors without the crunchy coating. If you want a little crispiness, grill a crispy surface on the meat side of the ribs before glazing. Raspberry adds a delicious twist!

2 slabs spareribs

Apple juice, for spraying (see page 13)

SAUCE

½ cup seedless raspberry jam

½ cup red wine vinegar

¼ cup soy sauce

¼ cup hoisin sauce

2 teaspoons Sriracha sauce

¼ cup minced scallion, both green and white parts

¼ cup peeled, finely minced fresh ginger

2 tablespoons sesame seeds, toasted

1 teaspoon ground coriander

½ teaspoon ground cinnamon

If possible, place each slab in a 2-gallon resealable plastic bag. If your slabs are very large, you may need to cut each slab in half and place each half in a separate bag so you'll have enough room for the marinade.

Combine all the ingredients for the sauce in a medium bowl and whisk. Set aside most of the sauce for grilling and serving. Brush the ribs evenly on both sides with a little of the sauce. Refrigerate for up to 8 hours.

Remove the ribs from the refrigerator. Heat a cooker to 250° to 275°F.

Oil the grate and place the unwrapped ribs on it bone side down over indirect heat. Cover and cook for 1½ hours. Spray with apple juice, turn, and cook for about 1½ hours more before turning and basting with apple juice again.

Cook for another 1 to 1½ hours, then test to see if the ribs are pull-apart tender. When tender, cook for 30 minutes longer, glazing the ribs with sauce every 10 minutes or as often as desired.

Transfer the ribs to a cutting board and let them rest, covered loosely with aluminum foil, for 10 to 15 minutes. While the ribs are resting, boil the remaining sauce for 1 to 2 minutes, if desired. Cut the ribs into individual pieces and serve with the sauce.

Smoked Spareribs with Cola Sauce

Serves 4 to 6

We have fond memories of swine dining years ago at the former Miss Piggy's Bar-B-Q on the outskirts of McPherson, Kansas. It wasn't much for decoration—the fanciest part of the décor being an assortment of gimme caps stapled to the walls. No matter the décor, we were there for the ribs. Part of what made them unique was the use of Coca-Cola in a special marinade. Although we haven't quite duplicated the flavor of Miss Piggy's here, we think you'll like these ribs. As the old saying or advertisement goes, things go better with Coke—even ribs.

RUB

⅓ cup paprika

¼ cup white cane sugar

3 tablespoons freshly ground black pepper

2 tablespoons salt

2 teaspoons dry mustard

2 teaspoons cayenne

1 teaspoon ground white pepper

RIBS

2 slabs spareribs

Apple juice, for spraying (see page 13)

SAUCE

2 cups cola

2 cups ketchup

½ cup white vinegar

¼ cup firmly packed dark brown sugar

2 teaspoons granulated onion

2 teaspoons salt

2 teaspoons freshly ground black pepper

1 teaspoon chili powder

1 teaspoon dry mustard

1 teaspoon ground allspice

½ teaspoon ground cinnamon

Combine all the ingredients for the rub in a small bowl and blend. Sprinkle the rub on the ribs, wrap tightly in plastic wrap, and refrigerate overnight.

Remove the ribs from the refrigerator. Heat a cooker to 250° to 275°F.

Oil the grate and place the unwrapped ribs on it bone side down over indirect heat. Cover and cook for 1½ hours, spray with apple juice, turn, and continue to cook for 1½ hours more before turning and spraying with apple juice again.

Meanwhile, combine all the ingredients for the sauce in a medium saucepan and bring to a boil over medium heat. Reduce the heat and simmer for 30 minutes, stirring occasionally. Set aside.

Cook for another 1 to 1½ hours, then test to see if the ribs are pull-apart tender. When tender, cook for 30 minutes longer, glazing the ribs with sauce every 10 minutes or as often as desired.

Transfer the ribs to a cutting board and let them rest, covered loosely with aluminum foil, for 10 to 15 minutes. While the ribs are resting, boil the remaining sauce for 1 to 2 minutes, if desired. Cut the ribs into individual pieces and serve with the sauce.

IT'S ALWAYS ALL ABOUT RIBS!

by Candy Weaver, owner of BBQr's Delight, Pine Bluff, Arkansas

In the big meats categories, I've always been fairly consistent, but ribs have long been my bane. The one and only time I took a first place in ribs was in Hot Springs, Arkansas, in 2008. That was actually my chicken year. Most every contest I cooked, I had a hit in chicken, except in Hot Springs. There was a hot-air balloon festival, lots of vendors, bands, motorcycles, and even a vintage car show. I'd purchased a sea-glass necklace at a vendor early on Saturday morning. She'd wished for some barbecue, and, of course, I said I'd take care of that. I thought my ribs that day were so bad. I cut all the leftovers up, bagged them, and took them to my jewelry-making friend. What a surprise it was when BBQr's Delight won first in ribs!

I'm still working hard to get that second first place in ribs! I came close with a third place once. As I write this, I'm heading to Oklahoma for another chance to stoke up the smoker and work toward the elusive Grand Champion award. For me, it's always all about ribs!

Smoked Mustard-Glazed Spareribs

Serves 2

Although many think mustard has been a secret ingredient in competition cooking for years, it actually was a traditional barbecue sauce in South Carolina long before it was discovered by competition cooks. Many contest teams slather their ribs with mustard as a marinade, while in South Carolina mustard is showcased front and center as a finishing sauce. This recipe uses mustard the way contest teams tend to use it: The mustard is hidden among other ingredients, but it adds a distinct sour note that rounds out the flavor. This is one of our favorite styles of ribs because we both like mustard sauces, especially on pork. The mustard brings out and complements the barbecue flavor.

1 slab spareribs

SAUCE

1¼ cups ketchup

⅓ cup apple cider vinegar

3 tablespoons prepared spicy brown mustard

2 tablespoons light brown sugar

3 tablespoons water

1 teaspoon onion powder

¼ teaspoon Louisiana hot sauce

Heat a cooker to 250° to 275°F.

Combine all the ingredients for the sauce in a small saucepan over medium heat. Simmer for 10 minutes. Divide the sauce in half and set aside both portions.

Oil the grate and place the ribs on it bone side down over indirect heat. Cover and cook for 1½ hours. Spray with apple juice, turn, and cook for about 1½ hours more before turning and basting with apple juice again.

Cook for another 1 to 1½ hours, then test to see if the ribs are pull-apart tender. When tender, cook for 30 minutes longer, glazing the ribs with sauce every 10 minutes or as often as desired.

Transfer the ribs to a cutting board and let them rest, covered loosely with aluminum foil, for 10 to 15 minutes. Cut the ribs into individual pieces and serve with the reserved sauce.

Grilled Peppered Dry Spareribs

Serves 4 to 6

These ribs get the benefit of a lemon pepper accent mixed with complementary seasonings and finished with an apple juice baste. We think they're best hot off the grill without any other seasonings. If you must, serve them with barbecue sauce on the side.

RUB

¼ cup white cane sugar

2 tablespoons lemon pepper

1 tablespoon onion salt

2 teaspoons celery salt

1 seasoned salt

1 tablespoon paprika

2 teaspoons Cajun seasoning (page 39, or your favorite)

1 teaspoon freshly ground black pepper

1 teaspoon ground coriander

½ teaspoon citric acid

RIBS

2 slabs spareribs

Apple juice, for spraying (see page 13)

Barbecue sauce, for serving (optional)

Heat a cooker to medium to medium-high.

Combine all the ingredients for the rub in a small bowl and blend. Rub all over the ribs.

Oil the grate and place the ribs on it bone side down over direct heat. Cover and cook for 2½ to 3½ hours, or until pull-apart tender, turning and spraying with apple juice every 10 to 15 minutes.

Transfer the ribs to a cutting board and let them rest, covered loosely with aluminum foil, for 10 to 15 minutes. Cut the ribs into individual pieces and serve with barbecue sauce.

Smoked Orange-Glazed Spareribs

Serves 4 to 6

These are in step with rib aficionados who like their ribs sweet. The orange accent makes them all the better.

RUB

2 tablespoons salt

1 tablespoon freshly ground black pepper

1 teaspoon granulated garlic

1 teaspoon white cane sugar

RIBS

2 slabs spareribs

Apple juice, for spraying (see page 13)

SAUCE

1 cup barbecue sauce

¼ cup clover or other mild-flavored honey

¼ cup fresh orange juice

2 tablespoons orange liqueur

1 teaspoon freshly grated orange zest

½ teaspoon crushed red pepper

Remove the ribs from the refrigerator. Heat a cooker to 250° to 275°F.

Combine all the ingredients for the rub in a small bowl and blend. Season the ribs all over with the rub.

Oil the grate and place the ribs on it bone side down over indirect heat. Cover and cook for 1½ hours, spray with apple juice, turn, and cook for about 1½ hours more before turning and spraying with apple juice again.

Meanwhile, combine all the ingredients for the sauce in a medium saucepan over medium heat. Bring to a boil, then reduce the heat and simmer for 15 minutes, stirring often. Set aside.

Cook or another 1 to 1½ hours test to see if the ribs are pull-apart tender. When tender, cook for 30 minutes longer, glazing the ribs with sauce every 10 minutes or as often as desired.

Transfer the ribs to a cutting board and let them rest, covered loosely with aluminum foil, for 10 to 15 minutes. Cut the ribs into individual pieces and serve.

Smoked Kansas City-Style Spareribs

Serves 8 to 10

Somehow Kansas Citians get stereotyped as preferring sweet, tomato-based sauces on their ribs. True, KC is the birthplace of the ever-popular KC Masterpiece barbecue sauces, but some of the most famous barbecue joints in town don't serve sweet sauce. This recipe fits the stereotype, but keep in mind that not all the ribs are sweet in Kansas City.

RUB

1½ cups white cane sugar

¼ cup salt

2½ tablespoons freshly ground black pepper

3 tablespoons paprika

2 tablespoons garlic salt

2 tablespoons onion salt

1 teaspoon cayenne

RIBS

4 slabs spareribs

Apple juice, for spraying (see page 13)

SAUCE

4 cups ketchup

2½ cups water

¼ cup molasses

¼ cup firmly packed light brown sugar

1 tablespoon crushed red pepper

1 teaspoon ground chipotle chile

1 tablespoon kosher salt

1 tablespoon coarsely ground black pepper

Combine all the ingredients for the rub in a medium bowl and blend. Rub all over the ribs. Place the ribs in two 10 by 15-inch roasting pans, two slabs per pan. Cover tightly with aluminum foil and refrigerate overnight.

Remove the ribs from the refrigerator. Heat a cooker to 250° to 275°F.

Oil the grate and place the ribs on it bone side down over indirect heat. Cover and cook for 1½ hours. Spray with apple juice, turn, and cook for about 1½ hours more before turning and spraying with apple juice again.

Meanwhile, combine all the ingredients for the sauce in a medium saucepan and bring to a boil over medium-high heat. Reduce the heat and simmer for 30 minutes, stirring occasionally.

Cook for another 1 to 1½ hours, then test to see if the ribs are pull-apart tender. When tender, cook for 30 minutes longer, glazing the ribs with sauce every 10 minutes or as often as desired.

Transfer the ribs to a cutting board and let them rest, covered loosely with aluminum foil, for 10 to 15 minutes. While the ribs are resting, boil the remaining sauce for 1 to 2 minutes, if desired. Cut the ribs into individual pieces and serve with the sauce.

Smoked Memphis-Style Spareribs

Serves 4 to 6

Chili powder in the rub and vinegar in the sauce make these ribs reminiscent of the "wet ribs" we've enjoyed in Memphis. Although some of the popular Memphis sauces include liquid smoke, you can omit it if you think the barbecue method of cooking yields enough authentic smoke flavor.

RUB

⅓ cup kosher salt

⅓ cup freshly ground black pepper

¼ cup dried dark brown sugar (see page 11)

2 tablespoons paprika

2 tablespoons ground chili powder

2 tablespoons cayenne

2 tablespoons ground cumin

2 tablespoons ground coriander

2 tablespoons Worcestershire powder (see Note)

1 tablespoon vinegar powder (see Note)

1 tablespoon ground ginger

RIBS

2 slabs spareribs

Apple juice, for spraying (see page 13)

SAUCE

2 cups ketchup

⅓ cup apple cider vinegar

¼ cup prepared yellow mustard

1 teaspoon liquid smoke (optional)

¼ cup firmly packed light brown sugar

Kosher salt

Freshly ground black pepper

Remove the ribs from the refrigerator. Heat a cooker to 250° to 275°F.

Combine all the ingredients for the rub in a medium bowl and blend. Rub all over the ribs.

Oil the grate and place the ribs on it bone side down over indirect heat. Cover and cook for 1½ hours. Spray with apple juice, turn, and cook for about 1½ hours more before turning and spraying with apple juice again.

Meanwhile, combine all the ingredients for the sauce in a medium saucepan and bring to a boil over medium-high heat. Reduce the heat and simmer for 10 to 15 minutes, stirring occasionally. Set aside.

Cook for another 1 to 1½ hours, then test to see if the ribs are pull-apart tender. When tender, cook for 30 minutes longer, glazing the ribs with sauce every 10 minutes or as often as desired.

Transfer the ribs to a cutting board and let them rest, covered loosely with aluminum foil, for 10 to 15 minutes. While the ribs are resting, boil the remaining sauce for 1 to 2 minutes, if desired. Cut the ribs into individual pieces and serve with the sauce.

Note: Worcestershire powder and vinegar powder are available from specialty spice retailers and online.

Smoked Spareribs with Red Currant Sauce

Serves 4 to 6

The balance of sweet and sour in these ribs makes for a good marriage. Great recipes for this combo abound. Chef Paul pulled this one from his archives and adapted it to our liking.

MARINADE

1 large sweet onion, such as Vidalia, minced or grated

2 large cloves garlic, pressed

¾ cup red currant jelly

¼ cup champagne vinegar

¼ cup clover or other mild-flavored honey

¼ cup light soy sauce

2 teaspoons peeled, grated fresh ginger

½ to 1 teaspoon Asian chili sauce

1 teaspoon Chinese five-spice powder

1 teaspoon salt

1 teaspoon freshly ground black pepper

RIBS

2 slabs spareribs

Apple juice, for spraying (see page 13)

Combine all the ingredients for the marinade in a medium bowl. If possible, place each slab in a 2-gallon resealable plastic bag. If your slabs are very large, you may need to cut each slab in half and place each half in a separate bag so you'll have enough room for the marinade. Pour the marinade over the ribs, seal the bag tightly, and turn gently to coat the ribs. Refrigerate for at least 30 minutes and up to overnight, turning occasionally.

Remove the ribs from the refrigerator. Heat a cooker to 250° to 275°F.

Remove the spareribs from the marinade and reserve the marinade. Oil the grate and place the ribs on it bone side down over indirect heat. Cover and cook for 1½ hours. Spray with apple juice, turn, and cook for about 1½ hours more before turning and spraying with apple juice again.

Meanwhile, transfer the reserved marinade to a small saucepan and bring it to a boil over medium-high heat. Reduce the heat and simmer for 2 to 3 minutes. Set aside.

Cook for another 1 to 1½ hours, then test to see if the ribs are pull-apart tender. When tender, cook for 30 minutes longer, glazing the ribs with the boiled marinade every 10 minutes or as often as desired.

Transfer the ribs to a cutting board and let them rest, covered loosely with aluminum foil, for 10 to 15 minutes. Cut the ribs into individual pieces and serve.

Smoked Spareribs with Maple Sauce

Serves 4 to 6

The sweet maple flavor in this recipe combined with some zing from lemon juice, lemon zest, and Worcestershire sauce resonates with any crowd of hungry rib eaters.

2 slabs spareribs

Garlic salt

Freshly ground black pepper

Apple juice, for spraying (see page 13)

SAUCE

2 cups ketchup

¾ cup grade B maple syrup

¼ cup fresh lemon juice

¼ cup firmly packed maple sugar
   or light brown sugar

2 tablespoons Worcestershire sauce

1 tablespoon soy sauce

1 teaspoon granulated garlic

1 teaspoon granulated onion

1 teaspoon freshly grated lemon zest

1 teaspoon ground coriander

1 teaspoon crushed red pepper

1 teaspoon salt

Remove the ribs from the refrigerator and season them all over with garlic salt and pepper. Heat a cooker to 250° to 275°F.

Oil the grate and place the ribs on it bone side down over indirect heat. Cover and cook for 1½ hours. Spray with apple juice, turn, and cook for about 1½ hours more before turning and basting with apple juice again.

Meanwhile, combine all the ingredients for the sauce in a medium saucepan over medium-low heat. Simmer, uncovered, for 15 to 20 minutes. Set aside.

Cook for an additional 1 to 1½ hours, then test to see if the ribs are pull-apart tender. When tender, cook for 30 minutes longer, glazing the ribs with sauce every 10 minutes or as often as desired.

Transfer the ribs to a cutting board and let them rest, covered loosely with aluminum foil, for 10 to 15 minutes. While the ribs are resting, boil the remaining sauce for 1 to 2 minutes, if desired. Cut the ribs into individual pieces and serve with the sauce.

Smoked Spareribs with Secret Glaze

Serves 4 to 6

One of Paul's aunts used to make meatballs or cocktail wieners with this wonderful barbecue sauce, calling it her "secret glaze." Paul later found out it's a recipe that has made the rounds at cocktail parties over the years, so it's not so secret, but we're including it here because it's so good—and great on ribs!

RUB

1 cup dried dark brown sugar (see page 11)

½ cup freshly ground black pepper

½ cup cayenne

3 tablespoons salt

1 tablespoon dry mustard

RIBS

2 slabs spareribs

Apple juice, for spraying (see page 13)

SAUCE

¾ cup chili sauce

½ cup grape jelly

2 teaspoons dry mustard

½ teaspoon ground chipotle chile

Remove the ribs from the refrigerator. Heat a cooker to 250° to 275°F.

Combine all the ingredients for the rub in a small bowl and blend. Season the ribs all over with the rub.

Oil the grate and place the ribs on it bone side down over indirect heat. Cover and cook for 1½ hours. Spray with apple juice, turn, and cook for about 1½ hours more before turning and spraying with apple juice again.

Meanwhile, combine all the ingredients for the sauce in a medium saucepan over medium-low heat. Heat until melted and well-combined, stirring occasionally. Set aside.

Cook for another 1 to 1½ hours, then test to see if the ribs are pull-apart tender. When tender, cook for 30 minutes longer, glazing the ribs with sauce every 10 minutes or as often as desired.

Transfer the ribs to a cutting board and let them rest, covered loosely with aluminum foil, for 10 to 15 minutes. While the ribs are resting, boil the remaining sauce for 1 to 2 minutes, if desired. Cut the ribs into individual pieces and serve with the sauce.

Islander Smoked Spareribs

Serves 4 to 6

What do you call a recipe that combines the flavors of Cuba, Hawaii, and Jamaica? We went with Islander Smoked Spareribs, but you can just call them "delicious!" As you savor these sweet and spicy spares, close your eyes and picture yourself having a barbecue on the beach while the waves roll out at sunset.

2 slabs spareribs

4 to 5 large cloves garlic, halved

Salt and freshly ground black pepper

Apple juice, for spraying (see page 13)

SAUCE

1 tablespoon granulated onion

1 (20-ounce) can crushed
   pineapple, undrained

1 (12-ounce) bottle chili sauce

½ cup firmly packed light brown sugar

2 tablespoons fresh lime juice

2 teaspoons ground ginger

1 teaspoon dry mustard

1 teaspoon ground allspice

1 teaspoon salt

½ teaspoon freshly ground white pepper

½ teaspoon ground habanero chile

¼ teaspoon cayenne

Remove the ribs from the refrigerator, rub them with garlic, and sprinkle with salt and pepper. Heat a cooker to 250° to 275°F.

Oil the grate and place the ribs on it bone side down over indirect heat. Cover and cook for 1½ hours. Spray with apple juice, turn, and cook for about 1½ hours more before turning and spraying with apple juice again.

Meanwhile, combine all the ingredients for the sauce in a medium saucepan over medium-high heat. Simmer for 15 to 20 minutes, stirring occasionally. Set aside.

Cook for an additional 1 to 1½ hours, then test to see if the ribs are pull-apart tender. When tender, cook for 30 minutes longer, glazing the ribs with sauce every 10 minutes, or as often as desired.

Transfer the ribs to a cutting board and let them rest, covered loosely with aluminum foil, for 10 to 15 minutes. While the ribs are resting, boil the remaining sauce for 1 to 2 minutes, if desired. Cut the ribs into individual pieces and serve with the sauce.

Senator Sumner's Smoked Spareribs

Serves 4 to 6

There are many variations of Yankee barbecued spareribs. Some are oven-baked with barbecue sauce. Some are boiled before being oven-baked in barbecue sauce. Some are smoked, sauced, and then wrapped in foil to steam until tender. Although our New England friends on the Bastey Boys team have bragging rights for calling their own version "Yankee," we hope they won't take issue with Chef Paul's rendition. We named it after a famous Civil War–era Yankee senator to prevent confusion with other recipes.

2 slabs spareribs

Salt

Lemon pepper

MOP

2 cups water

1 cup ketchup

½ cup apple cider vinegar

2 tablespoons Worcestershire sauce

¼ cup firmly packed light brown sugar

1 tablespoon granulated onion

1 teaspoon chili powder

1 teaspoon celery seeds

1 teaspoon cayenne

Heat a cooker to 250° to 275°F.

Season the ribs all over with salt and lemon pepper and set aside for about 1 hour.

Oil the grate and place the spareribs on it bone side down over indirect heat. Cover and smoke for 1½ hours.

Meanwhile, combine all the ingredients for the mop in a medium saucepan over medium heat and simmer for about 15 minutes.

Mop the ribs, turn, and cook for 1½ hours more before turning and mopping again. Cook for another 1 to 1½ hours, then test to see if the ribs are pull-apart tender. When tender, cook for 30 minutes longer, mopping the ribs every 10 minutes or as often as desired.

Transfer the ribs to a cutting board and let them rest, covered loosely with aluminum foil, for 10 to 15 minutes. While the ribs are resting, boil the remaining mop for 1 to 2 minutes. Cut the ribs into individual pieces and serve with the mop.

CHAPTER 3:

Beef & Bison Ribs

BEEF SHORT RIBS, BEEF BACK RIBS, and BISON RIBS

Ardie's dad, Art Davis, could tell a story with a straight face, a sparkle in his eye, and such perfect timing that you'd believe it even if you knew it was a joke. Some of his stories were true, like this one, about a swimming hole, a bull, and a hickory stick.

During Art's childhood, his mother, Nora, was kind and loving, but she had her rules, and there was a price to pay at the end of a hickory stick if you broke a rule. One of those rules was no swimming without adult supervision.

It was a hot summer day in the Missouri Ozarks. No adults were handy. Art couldn't resist. He went swimming. Noting his absence from the cabin, Nora caught on. Art had started to cool off and enjoy the swim when he saw Nora tromping through the woods with a scowl on her face. Naked, with pants in hand and running like a rabbit, he took a shortcut home, hoping Nora hadn't seen him. The shortcut would have worked if the bull in Farmer Pieland's pasture hadn't seen him. Art ran fast. The bull ran faster. Had it not been for the hedge apple tree in the pasture, Art wouldn't have lived to tell the story.

Nora had no fear. She marched right up to that tree, hickory stick in hand, and said, "Art Davis, you get yourself down here right this minute." He didn't know what hurt most—his pride or the stings from the hickory stick on the way home. There are bulls you avoid, and there are bulls you eat.

Grilled beef steaks and burgers have enjoyed enormous popularity on America's table for decades. Beef ribs, however, are most often featured in braised dishes instead of smoked or grilled. Bison burgers have long been popular, especially in restaurants. Not so with bison ribs. We know of only a few restaurants that serve them. We hope to inspire more Americans to enjoy beef and bison ribs with the ten easy recipes in this chapter. For best results in your bison ribs, we recommend using ribs from bison that are less than three years old. Meat from older bison is tougher, with less fat.

Before we get into the recipes, here are a few tips on the types of beef ribs. For information on selecting and prepping all types of ribs, see chapter 1.

Types and Cuts of Beef and Bison Ribs

Short ribs are the most common type of beef ribs. The best quality is off the plate, because they're meatier and less fatty than the ones off the chuck (flank).

As you'll see in the recipes in this chapter, we like to have our short ribs cut shorter across the bones. The bones in one whole slab of short ribs are 10 to 12 inches long, and the portions you cut from them are wide and thick. One whole bone with meat would be too big a portion for many people. That's why we cut them down, and many stores sell them packaged that way. The bones are too big and dense to cut yourself, so if they're not precut you'll have to ask your butcher or meat cutter to do it. One recipe in this chapter, for beef kalbi, calls for Korean (or flanken) cut ribs, which are short, delicious morsels that cook up in no time.

Back ribs are a full seven-bone slab. Some people feel that back ribs are easier to cook than short ribs, and they look big and impressive when you serve them.

Bison ribs are much like beef ribs, but they're bigger and have less fat.

The recipes in this chapter suggest that you take a sharp, pointed paring knife and outline the ribs with it. This helps the slathers, marinades, rubs, glazes, and even the smoke to better penetrate the thick, meaty rib meat. For a picture, see page 7.

Also note that beef ribs have a lot of fat that will burn quickly, so watch carefully for flare-ups and be ready to move the ribs back and forth over the cool zone as necessary.

Simple Smoked Beef Short Ribs

Serves 6

This simple recipe did not take the blue ribbon at any barbecue contest. It did come in third—by 2 points . . . in the Anything Butt Brisket category. In that category, you could barbecue anything but brisket and sirloin. Chef Paul chose to do beef short ribs, and almost everybody said he didn't have a chance of winning or even placing because he was going up against beef tenderloin, rib-eyes, T-bones, and porterhouse steaks. What did they know?!

6 (4- or 5-inch-long) beef short ribs

Barbecue sauce, for serving

MUSTARD SLATHER

1 cup prepared yellow mustard

¼ cup dill pickle juice

¼ cup red wine vinegar

2 tablespoons Worcestershire sauce

2 tablespoons soy sauce

1 teaspoon granulated garlic

1 teaspoon ground ginger

RUB

2 tablespoons sea salt

2 tablespoons coarse or restaurant grind black pepper

1 tablespoon granulated garlic

2 teaspoons white cane sugar

Remove the ribs from the refrigerator and outline the bones with a sharp, pointed paring knife.

Combine all the ingredients for the mustard slather in a small bowl and blend well. Brush the slather over the entire surface of the ribs.

Combine all the ingredients for the rub in a small bowl and blend well. Sprinkle the rub over the slathered ribs.

Heat a cooker to 230° to 250°F. Oil the rack and place the ribs on it bone side down over indirect heat. Cover and cook for 1 to 1½ hours. Turn and cook for 45 minutes more, then turn and cook for another 45 minutes, or until the ribs reach 185°F on a meat thermometer.

Transfer the ribs to a cutting board and let them rest, covered loosely with aluminum foil, for 10 to 15 minutes. Cut the ribs into individual pieces and serve with barbecue sauce.

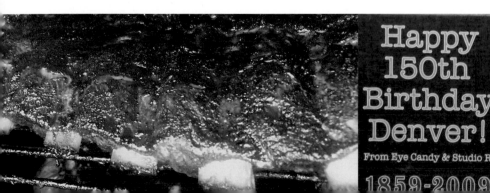

Happy 150th Birthday Denver!

From Eye Candy & Studio R

1859–2009

73

Jay's Tangy Grilled Beef Short Ribs

Serves 6

Paul's friend Jay makes these tangy, tender ribs. He got the recipe from a friend and tweaked it to suit his own taste.

6 (6-inch-long) beef short ribs

SAUCE

1 tablespoon granulated onion

2 teaspoons granulated garlic

1 (15-ounce) can diced
   tomatoes, undrained

½ cup cider vinegar

¼ cup balsamic vinegar

¼ cup firmly packed light brown sugar

½ cup ketchup

2 tablespoons prepared yellow mustard

2 tablespoons white cane sugar

½ teaspoon crushed dried basil

½ teaspoon ground coriander

½ teaspoon ground cumin

Remove the ribs from the refrigerator. Outline the bones with a sharp, pointed paring knife.

Combine all the ingredients for the sauce in a medium saucepan over medium heat. Bring it to a boil, then reduce the heat and simmer, uncovered, for 30 minutes, stirring occasionally. Cool the mixture, then puree it until smooth.

Place the ribs and 1 to 1½ cups of the sauce in a 2-gallon resealable plastic bag. Seal tightly and turn gently to completely coat the ribs. Refrigerate overnight and refrigerate the remaining sauce.

Remove the ribs from the refrigerator. Heat a cooker to medium-high.

Oil the grate and place the ribs on it bone side down over direct heat. Cover and cook for 1 to 1½ hours, or until the ribs reach 185°F on a meat thermometer, turning every 10 minutes and glazing with the reserved sauce during the last 30 minutes of cooking.

Transfer the ribs to a cutting board and let them rest, covered loosely with aluminum foil, for 10 to 15 minutes. While the ribs are resting, boil the remaining sauce for 1 to 2 minutes. Cut the ribs into individual pieces and serve with the sauce.

Korean-Style Grilled Beef Kalbi

Serves 6 to 8

This is Korean barbecue at its best: thin slices of beef short rib marinated and grilled. Korean-style beef short ribs are much thinner than the more common English version. They should only be about ¼ inch thick, with three rib bones attached. If you can't find them, other cuts of beef or ribs can be used (cooking times may vary).

MARINADE

½ cup pineapple juice

½ cup soy sauce

⅓ cup Asian malt syrup (see Notes)

4 scallions, both white and
    green parts, minced

4 medium cloves garlic, finely chopped

2 tablespoons dark sesame oil

2 tablespoons firmly packed
    light brown sugar

2 tablespoons soju liquor or
    light rum (see Notes)

½ teaspoon freshly ground black pepper

RIBS

3 to 4 pounds Korean-style (flanken
    cut) beef short ribs (see Notes)

1 tablespoon toasted sesame
    seeds, for garnish

Combine all the ingredients for the marinade in a medium bowl and whisk to blend. Place the ribs in a 2-gallon resealable plastic bag, pour in the marinade, seal tightly, and turn gently to coat the ribs completely. Refrigerate for at least 12 hours and up to overnight.

Remove the ribs from the refrigerator. Heat a cooker to high and oil the grate.

Remove the ribs from the marinade and discard the marinade. Place the ribs on the grate, spaced 1 inch apart. Cover and cook until well-done and crispy on the edges, about 5 minutes per side (watch for flare-ups).

Transfer the ribs to a serving platter, sprinkle with sesame seeds, and serve.

Notes: Asian malt syrup and soju liquor can be purchased at Asian markets. You also can substitute light molasses for the Asian malt syrup.

Korean-style, or flanken cut, short ribs are cut ¼ to ½ inch thick across the ribs. Ask your butcher or meat cutter for them.

75

West Bottoms Glazed Smoked Beef Short Ribs

Serves 8

Kansas City's West Bottoms is the former home of the famous Kansas City Stockyards, which were a major factor in the birth of barbecue as a citywide passion. Today the area is home to the world's largest barbecue contest, the American Royal. A variety of old and new popular eating places attract urban foodies, as well. These wine-marinated ribs aren't on local menus, but the ingredients are reminiscent of the area's diverse past and present. Enjoy these ribs with a glass of dry red wine and give a toast to Kansas City's past, present, and future!

8 (6-inch-long) beef short ribs

Barbecue sauce, for glazing

MARINADE

½ cup dry red wine

¼ cup soy sauce

2 tablespoons canola oil

2 tablespoons Worcestershire sauce

2 tablespoons fresh lemon juice

3 cloves garlic, pressed

½ teaspoon crushed dried thyme

½ teaspoon freshly ground black pepper

Remove the ribs from the refrigerator and outline them with a sharp, pointed paring knife.

Combine all the ingredients for the marinade in a medium bowl and blend well. Place the ribs in a 2-gallon resealable plastic bag, pour in the marinade, seal tightly, and turn gently to coat the ribs completely. Refrigerate for at least 2 hours and up to overnight.

Remove the ribs from the refrigerator. Heat a cooker to 230° to 250°F and oil the grate.

Remove the ribs from the marinade and discard the marinade. Place the ribs on the grate bone side down over indirect heat. Cover and cook for 1 to 1½ hours. Turn and cook for 45 minutes more, then turn and cook for another 45 minutes, or until the ribs reach 185°F on a meat thermometer, glazing the ribs with barbecue sauce every 10 minutes during the last 30 minutes of cooking.

Transfer the ribs to a cutting board and let them rest, covered loosely with aluminum foil, for 10 to 15 minutes. Cut the ribs into individual pieces and serve with the remaining barbecue sauce.

IT'S ALL ABOUT THE TIMING!

by Clint Cantwell, Smoke in da Eye competition barbecue team

cooked at a contest with or against me can attest, I tend to push the limits of the turn-in clock more times than I'd care to admit. New Holland Summerfest 2010 was different, though. My site was situated no more than 10 feet from the turn-in table, and with two additional categories to do that day, I made sure I was ahead of schedule. Chicken went in, and as twelve thirty began to approach I sliced the ribs and put them in the box. I had decided to cook baby backs this time, having had subpar results with spares the last few times out, and they looked great. I cleaned up the box, and my dad closed the lid . . . hard. The tabs broke off and the lid popped open. As it turns out, the box was a little shallower than the ones I had used in the past, and the ribs were sitting a bit too high on the garnish. The team offered me a box from one of the other categories, but I was determined to reposition the ribs so the lid would close. (In my mind it was easier than building another box of garnish.) I got the ribs situated lower and looked at the clock to see that I still had 90 seconds or so to make it 10 feet, so I closed the lid. One problem. The lid still had no tabs to keep it closed. So I called for another box, got the ribs in and looking great within seconds, and stepped out with 15 to 20 seconds left. Suddenly someone stepped between me and the turn-in table, I spun around him, set down my box, and . . . I was 1 second late. Fortunately, I wasn't in the running for Grand Champion that day, but the experience hurt. It did, however, teach me to be a little smarter the next time an issue like that arises. I also learned a valuable lesson in both competition and life: Get over the frustration quickly and get back to the task at hand—in that case, pork shoulder, followed by brisket.

Be-Back Sweet Smoked Beef Short Ribs

Serves 8

Artists at art fairs have a label for browsers who say, "I'll be back," as they leave the booth. "Be-Backs" seldom return. These ribs are a work of art. The sweet, smoky, meaty, rich flavor will compel most of your guests to be back for more!

8 (6-inch-long) beef short ribs

SAUCE

1 cup tomato sauce

1 cup barbecue sauce

¼ cup cola

2 tablespoons clover or other
  mild-flavored honey

2 tablespoons firmly packed
  dark brown sugar

2 tablespoons apple cider vinegar

1 teaspoon ground oregano

½ teaspoon ground thyme

½ teaspoon white pepper

¼ teaspoon Louisiana hot sauce

1 teaspoon granulated garlic

RUB

⅓ cup firmly packed light brown sugar

1 tablespoon paprika

2 teaspoon sea salt

1 teaspoon white pepper

1 teaspoon finely ground black pepper

1 teaspoon cayenne

Heat a cooker to 230° to 250°F. Remove the ribs from the refrigerator and outline them with a sharp, pointed paring knife.

Combine all the ingredients for the sauce in a medium saucepan. Bring it to a boil over medium heat, then reduce the heat and simmer for 5 minutes. If the sauce is too thick to brush on the ribs, add water to thin, as desired. Set aside.

Combine all the ingredients for the rub in a small bowl and blend well. Season the ribs all over with the rub.

Oil the grate and place the ribs on it bone side down over indirect heat. Cover and cook for 1 to 1½ hours. Turn and cook for 45 minutes more, then turn and cook for another 45 minutes, or until the ribs reach 185°F on a meat thermometer, glazing the ribs with the sauce every 10 minutes during the last 30 minutes of cooking.

Transfer the ribs to a cutting board and let them rest, covered loosely with aluminum foil, for 10 to 15 minutes. While the ribs are resting, boil the remaining sauce for 1 to 2 minutes. Cut the ribs into individual pieces and serve with the sauce.

Honey and Molasses Smoked Beef Back Ribs

Serves 6 to 8

The dry rub and extra-sweet sauce in this recipe lend a peppery sweet balance to these ribs. Remember to have wet washcloths handy for each guest. Their hands and mouths will be saucy, and their exclamations will be, "Delicious!" You can honestly reply, "Thanks. It was easy."

2 slabs beef back ribs

RUB

2 tablespoons granulated garlic

2 tablespoons ground cumin

2 tablespoons mild chili powder

3 tablespoons dark brown sugar

3 tablespoons coarse or restaurant grind black pepper

3 tablespoons sea salt

1 tablespoon cayenne

SAUCE

½ cup barbecue sauce

¼ cup clover or other mild-flavored honey

¼ cup molasses

¼ cup blue agave syrup

¼ cup fresh lime juice

2 tablespoons ground cumin

2 tablespoons ground coriander

Heat a cooker to 230° to 250°F. Remove the ribs from the refrigerator and outline them with a sharp, pointed paring knife.

Combine all the ingredients for the rub in a small bowl and blend well. Season the ribs all over with the rub.

Oil the grate and place the ribs on it bone side down over indirect heat. Cover and cook for 1 to 1½ hours.

Meanwhile, combine all the ingredients for the sauce in a medium bowl and blend well.

Turn the ribs and cook for 45 minutes more, then turn and cook for another 45 minutes, or until pull-apart tender, glazing the ribs with the sauce every 10 minutes during the last 30 minutes of cooking.

Transfer the ribs to a cutting board and let them rest, covered loosely with aluminum foil, for 10 to 15 minutes. While the ribs are resting, boil the remaining sauce for 1 to 2 minutes. Cut the ribs into individual pieces and serve with the sauce.

Texas Cowgirls Smoked Beef Back Ribs

Serves 6 to 8

Bandera, Texas, is our favorite cowgirl town. It's a place where you can get good barbecue, attend a cabrito festival contest, and meet some very interesting authentic Texans. The local cowgirls are so sassy they even have a toilet paper named after them. These ribs aren't as sassy as the Bandera Cowgirls, but they'll bite you with cayenne and green chiles, then sweeten your palate with honey. Sort of a cowgirl metaphor is how we think of it.

2 slabs beef back ribs

RUB

2 tablespoons sea salt

1 tablespoon finely ground black pepper

1 teaspoon granulated garlic

1 teaspoon cayenne

SAUCE

½ cup ketchup

½ cup clover or other
   mild-flavored honey

1 (4-ounce) can diced green chiles

2 teaspoons granulated onion

1 teaspoon granulated garlic

1 teaspoon mild chili powder

1 teaspoon dry mustard

1 teaspoon salt

1 teaspoon freshly ground black pepper

½ teaspoon ground chipotle chile

Heat a cooker to 230° to 250° F. Remove the ribs from the refrigerator and outline them with a sharp, pointed paring knife.

Combine all the ingredients for the rub in a small bowl and blend well. Season the ribs all over with the rub.

Oil the grate and place the ribs on it bone side down over indirect heat. Cover and cook for 1 to 1½ hours.

Combine all the ingredients for the sauce in a medium saucepan over low heat. Cook, stirring, until warm.

Turn the ribs and cook for 45 minutes more, then turn and cook for another 45 minutes, or until pull-apart tender, glazing every 10 minutes during the last 30 minutes, or as desired, until you get a thick coating.

Transfer the ribs to a cutting board and let them rest, covered loosely with aluminum foil, for 10 to 15 minutes. While the ribs are resting, boil the remaining sauce for 1 to 2 minutes. Cut the ribs into individual pieces and serve with the sauce.

Texas-Style Smoked Beef Back Ribs

Serves 6 to 8

When your roundup is over, however you may define it, these smoked ribs with barbecue sauce and a pot of pinto beans spiced with jalapeño chiles are a perfect way to celebrate. Though it's better to provide dining tables and chairs for the comfort of your guests, if you want to be true to nineteenth-century cowboy tradition, you and your guests can sit on the ground near your barbecue pit and use your laps or the ground as your dining table.

2 slabs beef back ribs

Barbecue sauce, for serving

RUB

2 tablespoons freshly ground black pepper

1 tablespoon ground oregano

1 tablespoon paprika

1 tablespoon salt

2 teaspoons celery salt

1 teaspoon granulated garlic

1 teaspoon cayenne

Heat a cooker to 230° to 250°F. Remove the ribs from the refrigerator and outline them with a sharp, pointed paring knife.

Combine all the ingredients for the rub in a small bowl and blend well. Season the ribs all over with the rub.

Oil the grate and place the ribs on it bone side down over indirect heat. Cover and cook for 1 to 1½ hours. Turn and cook for 45 minutes more, then turn and cook for another 45 minutes, or until pull-apart tender.

Transfer the ribs to a cutting board and let them rest, covered loosely with aluminum foil, for 10 to 15 minutes. Cut the ribs into individual pieces and serve with barbecue sauce.

Smoked Bison Back Ribs

Serves 4

One of our favorite images of the romanticized American West of the nineteenth century is a watercolor by Alfred Jacob Miller depicting six trappers gathered around an evening campfire. One is holding a skewered slab of bison hump ribs, smoking and grilling over the fire and smoke. Miller deemed bison hump ribs to be "that most glorious of all mountain morsels." Today the bison hump is sold as a boneless roast. Most vendors sell bison short ribs or back ribs, with no references to hump ribs. Channel your inner Old West trapper spirit anyway and prepare these back ribs with this easy basic recipe, which we believe would bring a delighted smile to Alfred Jacob Miller's face.

1 slab bison back ribs

Barbecue sauce, for serving

RUB

1 tablespoon lemon pepper

1 tablespoon garlic salt

1 teaspoon cayenne

½ teaspoon ground rosemary

¼ teaspoon ground thyme

Heat a cooker to 230° to 250°F. Remove the ribs from the refrigerator and outline them with a sharp, pointed paring knife.

Combine all the ingredients for the rub in a small bowl and blend well. Season the ribs all over with the rub.

Oil the grate and place the ribs on it bone side down over indirect heat. Cover and cook for 1 to 1½ hours. Turn and cook for 45 minutes more, then turn and cook for another 45 minutes, or until pull-apart tender.

Increase the heat to 350° to 400°F. Glaze the ribs with the sauce and cook for 5 to 7 minutes, being careful not to burn the ribs, then turn and glaze again and cook for another 5 to 7 minutes. Repeat 2 or 3 times, if desired.

Transfer the ribs to a cutting board and let them rest, covered loosely with aluminum foil, for 10 to 15 minutes. Cut the ribs into individual pieces and serve with barbecue sauce.

Righteous Urban Grilled and Smoked Buffalo Ribs

Serves 4

If you carry pocket change, there's a good chance you have at least one bison in your pocket—the 2005 Jefferson nickel with an American bison on the tails side. In honor of our Founding Fathers and their righteous cause, liberty, Chef Paul has developed this recipe, which calls for five seasoning ingredients and five easy steps to cook to perfection.

1 slab bison back ribs

Barbecue sauce, for serving

RUB

1 tablespoon freshly ground black pepper

2 teaspoons garlic salt

1 teaspoon onion salt

1 teaspoon crushed dried thyme

1 teaspoon ground chipotle chile

Heat a grill to medium-high for direct cooking and a smoker to 230° to 250°F for indirect cooking. Remove the ribs from the refrigerator and outline them with a sharp, pointed paring knife.

Combine all the ingredients for the rub in a small bowl and blend well. Season the ribs all over with the rub.

Oil the grill grate and place the ribs on it bone side down over direct heat. Grill for 5 to 7 minutes per side, or until the ribs develop a browned and crispy crust, 40 to 45 minutes.

Oil the smoker grate and transfer the ribs to it bone side down over indirect heat. Cover and cook for 1 to 1½ hours. Turn and cook for 45 minutes more, then turn and cook for another 45 minutes, or until pull-apart tender.

Transfer the ribs to a cutting board and let them rest, covered loosely with aluminum foil, for 10 to 15 minutes. Cut the ribs into individual pieces and serve with barbecue sauce.

CHAPTER 4:

Lamb
&Mutton
Ribs

LAMB BREAST RIBS, DENVER RIBS, MUTTON BREAST RIBS

Paul comes from a large family known for celebrating holidays and birthdays with family barbecues. When they were celebrating his mother's eighty-second birthday, it was Paul's turn to entertain his mother and his five sisters' and brothers' families. They usually would barbecue ribs and chicken and serve them with potato salad, made-from-scratch baked beans, garlic bread, deviled eggs, and strawberry shortcake along with birthday cake.

That year Paul got the great idea to buy a case of Denver lamb ribs and barbecue them as a treat for everyone. He spent most of the day barbecuing a case of spareribs, a case of Denver lamb ribs, and ten chickens. He cut everything up and put them all in their respective serving pans and said, "Come and get it."

Of course, Paul's mother went first after all the little kids' plates were fixed. Paul watched her go through the line and noticed that she didn't take any lamb ribs. He asked her, "Don't you want any lamb?" A quick answer came back, "NO! I don't like lamb. The only reason we had lamb on Easter is that your father insisted on it because it was traditional to serve lamb then!" Paul was shocked, to say the least. Until that day he had not known his mother did not care for lamb. Paul himself loves lamb and has since he was a little person, remembering those Easter treats.

We're not sure why Paul's mom hated lamb, but some people avoid lamb and mutton because they expect a distasteful strong flavor. We've tasted that strong flavor, and while it doesn't disagree with us, we'd rather enjoy lamb and mutton without it. It is easily done, as you'll see when you follow our recipes in this chapter.

Some cooks like to cook the ribs and breast together as one piece. Others prefer the ribs separated from the breast. The breast can be cut into spareribs or riblets. With breasts, what you gain in a lower price you lose in the amount of fat you'll need to trim. Ask your butcher for the cut you want.

Lamb ribs come from young sheep. Mutton ribs come from older sheep—or, as the Bosley family in Daviess County, Kentucky, says, "older, wiser lambs." Spring lambs have little or no gamy flavor. Winter lambs usually will have a gamy flavor, and mutton for sure will have it. Regardless of the age of the animal, using the cooking techniques in this chapter will minimize or eliminate gamy flavor and bring out that rich, delicious taste.

In barbecue joints, lamb ribs tend to be a gourmet item. Mutton ribs are the working person's ribs. They are common in Kentucky barbecue joints. While they are not as widely available elsewhere, we have enjoyed them in central Texas, Georgia, and Tennessee (where more than one community has a Mutton Hollow Road). Mutton ribs were once found in several Kansas City barbecue joints, but not today. With the passing of Otis Boyd—who barbecued some of the most memorable mutton breast with ribs we've ever eaten—one of the few places we can still find barbecued mutton ribs in Kansas City is at Gates Bar-B-Q. When we're hungry for lamb ribs, we go directly to Fiorella's Jack Stack Barbecue, or we smoke our own.

If you're a fan of lamb or mutton ribs, you're not limited to finding a barbecue joint that serves them. We offer you some classics here with our own favorite flavors and touches to make you a jumbuck (Australian slang for sheep) pitmaster par excellence.

Before we get into the recipes, here are a few tips on the types of lamb and mutton ribs. For information on selecting and prepping all types of ribs, see Chapter 1.

FIG. 187. Parts of the sheep.

1. Forehead	8. Rump	15. Belly
2. Face	9. Dock	16. Fore flank
3. Neck	10. Thigh	17. Fore leg
4. Top of shoulder	11. Twist	18. Breast
5. Back	12. Pastern	19. Shoulder
6. Loin	13. Foot	20. Ribs
7. Hip	14. Rear flank	

Types and Cuts of Lamb and Mutton Ribs

Lamb breast ribs come as a full slab of lamb ribs, with 9 to 12 bones. They are sold by weight, and they vary in size. Restaurants often just call them *lamb breast*. They tend to be fatty and somewhat tough, but you can trim off excess fat.

Denver ribs are a slab of lamb breast ribs that has been squared off at the small end, usually contains 7 to 8 ribs, and weighs 1 to 2 pounds. A slab of Denver ribs is to a slab of lamb breast ribs as a St. Louis–style slab of pork ribs is to a full slab of pork spareribs (see page 24).

Mutton breast ribs are breast ribs from a grown-up animal. They can be larger than lamb breast ribs, though not always. They have a stronger flavor than lamb.

88

Bob's Sweet-and-Sour Grilled Jumbuck Ribs

Serves 6 to 8

This one honors our longtime barbecue buddy, the late Bob Carruthers, of New South Wales. We met Bob during his first trip to Lynchburg, Tennessee, to serve as an international judge at the Jack Daniel's World Championship Invitational Barbecue. From then on he played a significant role in introducing Australian barbecue to Americans and American barbecue to Australians. His footprints on The Jack will endure, as will many good memories of the fun and enthusiasm he brought to the event. For this one we recommend Australian lamb ribs, and the whiskey has to be Jack Daniel's. Life is sweet. Life is sour. Life goes on.

6 slabs Denver lamb ribs

1 tablespoon olive oil

Salt and freshly ground black pepper

GLAZE

½ cup pineapple juice

¼ cup white wine vinegar

2 tablespoons soy sauce

¼ cup ketchup

2 tablespoons dark brown sugar

1 tablespoon peeled, minced fresh ginger

2 tablespoons fresh lime juice

1 tablespoon minced fresh cilantro leaves

1 tablespoon minced fresh mint leaves

Heat a cooker to medium to medium-high. Rub the ribs all over with the olive oil, then season with salt and pepper.

To make the glaze, combine the pineapple juice, vinegar, and soy sauce in a small saucepan over medium heat. Cook until reduced by half, about 3 to 5 minutes. Add the ketchup, brown sugar, and ginger and simmer for 5 minutes. Stir in the lime juice, cilantro, and mint. Remove from the heat and set aside.

Oil the grate and place the ribs on it bone side down over direct heat. Cook for 5 to 7 minutes, then turn and cook for 5 to 7 minutes more. Repeat the process for 40 to 45 minutes, or until the ribs are pull-apart tender. Move the ribs away from direct heat and glaze the bone side with sauce, then turn and glaze the meat side. Cook for 10 minutes. Repeat one or two more times, if desired.

Transfer the ribs to a cutting board and let them rest, covered loosely with aluminum foil, for 10 to 15 minutes. Cut the ribs into individual pieces and serve.

Whiskey River Grilled Lamb Ribs

Serves 2 to 4

What's not to like about America's favorite outlaw icon balladeer, Willie Nelson? We know he likes pork ribs (see page 110), and we sure do hope he likes these lamb ribs with Texas and Tennessee accents. Ribs to ya, Willie!

MUSTARD SLATHER

⅓ cup Dijon mustard

2 tablespoons fresh lemon juice

RUB

2 teaspoons garlic salt

1 teaspoon lemon pepper

1 teaspoon freshly ground black pepper

1 teaspoon ground cumin

1 teaspoon paprika

¼ teaspoon ground chipotle chile

RIBS

2 slabs lamb breast ribs

SAUCE

1 (15-ounce) can tomato puree

1 (8-ounce) can tomato sauce

⅓ cup red wine vinegar

½ cup molasses

½ cup firmly packed light brown sugar

½ cup diced applewood-smoked bacon

3 tablespoons chopped chipotles in adobo

1 tablespoon granulated onion

2 teaspoons ground cumin

Salt and freshly ground black pepper

½ cup Jack Daniel's or your favorite whiskey

To make the slather, combine the mustard and lemon juice in a small bowl and blend well. Set aside.

Combine all the ingredients for the rub in another small bowl and blend well. Set aside.

Brush the mustard slather over the bone side of the ribs, then season them with some rub. Repeat on the meat side. Wrap tightly in plastic and refrigerate overnight.

Remove the ribs from the refrigerator.

To make the sauce, combine the tomato puree, tomato sauce, vinegar, brown sugar, molasses, bacon, chopped chipotles, granulated onion, cumin, and salt and pepper to taste in a large saucepan over low heat. Cook for 1 hour, stirring occasionally. Set aside to cool, then puree the mixture in a blender. Stir in the whiskey. Set aside.

Heat a cooker to medium to medium-high.

Oil the grate and place the ribs on it bone side down over direct heat. Cook for 5 to 7 minutes, then turn and cook for 5 to 7 minutes more. Repeat the process for 40 to 45 minutes, or until the ribs are pull-apart tender. Move the ribs away from direct heat and glaze the bone side with sauce, then turn and glaze the meat side. Cook for 10 minutes. Repeat one or two more times, if desired.

Transfer the ribs to a cutting board and let them rest, covered loosely with aluminum foil, for 10 to 15 minutes. Cut the ribs into individual pieces and serve.

Phyllis and Leo's Smoked Luau Lamb Ribs

Serves 6 to 8

Ardie's parents-in-law, Phyllis and Leo Mueller, loved Hawaii so much that they vacationed there at least a dozen times. Leo has passed away, but Phyllis is still going strong and celebrated her 97th birthday with a luau party in the Buffalo Lake, Minnesota, Healthcare Center. We wish we could have served her party of 150-plus celebrants these delicious Hawaiian-flavored ribs!

MARINADE

½ cup soy sauce

½ cup pineapple juice

¼ cup hoisin sauce

¼ cup seasoned rice vinegar

2 tablespoons clover or other mild-flavored honey

2 tablespoons white cane sugar

2 tablespoons peanut oil

4 cloves garlic, pressed

2 teaspoons crushed red pepper

1 teaspoon salt

1 teaspoon freshly ground black pepper

1 teaspoon red food coloring (optional)

RIBS

6 slabs Denver lamb ribs

SALSA

1 cup crushed pineapple

½ cup diced fresh mango

¼ cup diced red onion

2 tablespoons minced fresh parsley

1 teaspoon cayenne

1 teaspoon salt

Combine all the ingredients for the marinade in a medium bowl and whisk to blend. Place the ribs in a 2-gallon resealable plastic bag. Pour the marinade into the bag, seal tightly, and turn gently to completely coat the ribs. Refrigerate for at least 4 hours and up to overnight, turning occasionally.

Remove the ribs from the refrigerator. Heat a cooker to 230° to 250°F.

Remove the ribs from the marinade and transfer the marinade to a small saucepan. Bring it to a boil over high heat. Reduce the heat and simmer for 2 to 3 minutes. Set aside.

Oil the grate and place the ribs on it bone side down over indirect heat. Cover and cook for 1½ to 2½ hours, turning and basting with some of the reserved marinade every 45 minutes, until pull-apart tender.

While the ribs are cooking, combine all the ingredients for the salsa in a medium bowl and mix well.

Transfer the ribs to a cutting board and let them rest, covered loosely with aluminum foil, for 10 to 15 minutes. Cut the ribs into individual pieces and serve with the salsa.

MAKING THE BEST OF IT

by Jessica Kirk, First Kansas State Barbecue Champion

In the summer of 1985, I competed in the one and only Liberty Memorial Barbecue Contest.

There were lots of things going on that weekend on the hill. A musical festival of some sort was taking place, there were activities for families, and some branch of the military was spending lots of time flying over the scene in helicopters.

My "team" consisted of my three kids and me. Todd was ten, Chris was eight, and Erin was five. While we set up our site, their dad, Chef Paul, already a professional, could not be near our camp for fear of people thinking he might be helping me. We were just about finished getting things set up, and I was pounding the last stake in the ground for our dining/sun shade fly (this was before pop-up tents). The helicopter came over again, and everyone started waving and hollering. At that point the guys in the copter came down for a closer look at the ground forces. Yep, you guessed it. Tables, chairs, and cooking materials went flying everywhere. As each child grabbed a pole, the dining fly took off like a kite with three tails (my kids) tumbling after it. The contest was not off to a good start.

After retrieving most of our supplies and up-righting the fifty-five–gallon drum we used for cooking, we got rolling again. The cooking process was going well, and the night progressed without further incident. The light of day was another matter. About three hours before turn-in time there was a "small" fire due to a dry water pan. My ribs were somewhat "charred," and in my mind they were headed for the dog bowl. My husband had always said "Never give up and don't forget the apple juice," so I sprayed the ribs with apple juice, double-wrapped them in plastic wrap, and tossed them in an empty cooler. When it was time, the ribs were sliced and presented for judging. At least we had something to turn in, I thought, and maybe our other entries would do well.

When awards were announced, we were stunned. Not only had our other entries placed well, but our ribs had taken first place! We ended up taking Grand Champion!

Tuscan Smoked Lamb Ribs

Serves 2 to 4

Gabrielle Hamilton, chef/proprietor of Prune, a small, enormously popular restaurant in New York City, told a story in the *New Yorker* magazine called "The Lamb Roast: What Was Cooking at Our Place," which caught our attention and made us wish we had been there when her dad roasted whole lambs over green applewood in a pit. Gabrielle didn't share her dad's lamb recipe, but she said enough about the baste to inspire Chef Paul's adaptation of this fabulous recipe for barbecue breast of lamb with the flavors of Tuscany. This one's for our good friend, the late Giancarlo Giannelli, Barbecue Baron of Tuscany.

MARINADE

1 cup fresh lemon juice

⅓ cup olive oil

3 cloves garlic, pressed

¼ cup grated yellow onion

1 teaspoon minced fresh rosemary

1 teaspoon salt

½ teaspoon freshly ground black pepper

RIBS

2 slabs lamb breast ribs

Barbecue sauce, for serving

Combine all the ingredients for the marinade in a small bowl and blend well. Place the ribs in a 2-gallon resealable plastic bag. Pour the marinade into the bag, seal tightly, and turn gently to completely coat the ribs. Refrigerate for 1 hour.

Remove the ribs from the refrigerator. Heat a cooker to 230° to 250°F.

Oil the grate and place the ribs on it bone side down over indirect heat. Cover and cook for 1½ to 2½ hours, turning every 45 minutes, until pull-apart tender.

Transfer the ribs to a cutting board and let them rest, covered loosely with aluminum foil, for 10 to 15 minutes. Cut the ribs into individual pieces and serve with barbecue sauce.

Grilled Tandoori Lamb Ribs

Serves 2 to 4

Besides imparting a distinctive orange-red patina to grilled meat, the tandoori seasonings in this recipe add a spicy, zesty flavor to grilled lamb breasts that is one of our favorite flavor combos.

2 tablespoons cumin seeds

1 tablespoon garam marsala
  or curry powder

2 teaspoons fennel seeds

2 teaspoons cardamom seeds

½ teaspoon whole black peppercorns

1½ teaspoons crushed red pepper

6 tablespoons olive oil

2 tablespoon peeled, minced fresh ginger

4 garlic cloves, pressed

2 slabs lamb breast ribs

Combine the cumin, garam masala or curry powder, fennel, cardamom, and peppercorns in a small, dry skillet over medium heat and toast until aromatic, 2 to 3 minutes. Let cool, then combine with the crushed red pepper in a spice mill and grind. Transfer the spice blend to a small bowl and stir in the olive oil, ginger, and garlic.

Rub the spice paste all over the ribs, then wrap in plastic and refrigerate for at least 3 hours and up to overnight.

Remove the ribs from the refrigerator. Heat a cooker to medium to medium-high.

Oil the grate and place the ribs on it bone side down over direct heat. Cook for 5 to 7 minutes, then turn and cook for 5 to 7 minutes more. Repeat the process for 40 to 45 minutes, or until the ribs are pull-apart tender.

Transfer the ribs to a cutting board and let them rest, covered loosely with aluminum foil, for 10 to 15 minutes. Cut the ribs into individual pieces and serve.

Joellyn's Smoked Mutton Breast

Serves 2 to 4

Joellyn Sullivan is co-proprietor of the famous Silky O'Sullivan's on Beale Street in Memphis, where pizza, oysters, barbecue sandwiches, Cajun sandwiches, po' boys, barbecue ribs, and other foods are consumed indoors and outdoors to the tunes of guest musicians in a yearlong St. Patrick's Day scene. Her husband and co-proprietor, Silky, is an international barbecue rock star. They are longtime friends and Barbecue Royalty. Joellyn was kind enough to share this recipe with us, a variation on the recipe she gave to Chef Paul for leg of lamb at the World Cup Barbecue Championship years ago in Lisdoonvarna, Ireland, where she took home the blue ribbon for lamb in 1989.

2 slabs mutton breast ribs

¼ cup olive oil

1 tablespoon granulated garlic

3 tablespoons lemon pepper

2 teaspoons crushed dried rosemary

Heat a cooker to 230° to 250°F.

Remove the ribs from the refrigerator and rub them all over with the olive oil. Sprinkle with the granulated garlic, then season with the lemon pepper and rosemary.

Oil the grate and place the ribs on it bone side down over indirect heat. Cover and cook for 1½ to 2½ hours, turning every 45 minutes, until the ribs are pull-apart tender.

Transfer the ribs to a cutting board and let them rest, covered loosely with aluminum foil, for 10 to 15 minutes. Cut the ribs into individual pieces and serve.

Silky O'Sullivan' World Famous Ribs

Texas Desperados Grilled Mutton Ribs

Serves 2 to 4

We love Texas cuisine and Texas music. One of our favorite country-western songs out of Texas is Guy Clark's "Desperados Waiting for a Train." Our esteemed barbecue buddy John Raven, PhB, says, "Although Texas raises many, many lambs, they just don't fit the Texas idea of stick-to-your-ribs food. Lamb may not be hearty fare, but it is delicious, and it lends itself wonderfully to grilling." John uses all of the ingredients in this recipe when he grills mutton or lamb. Don't mess with Texas.

RUB

2 tablespoons kosher salt

2 tablespoons coarsely
   ground black pepper

1 tablespoon dried minced garlic

1 tablespoon crushed dried rosemary

1 teaspoon cayenne

1 teaspoon coarsely ground cumin

RIBS

2 slabs mutton breast ribs

Heat a cooker to medium to medium-high.

Combine all the ingredients for the rub in a small bowl and blend well. Season the ribs all over with the rub.

Oil the grate and place the ribs on it bone side down over direct heat. Cook for 5 to 7 minutes, then turn and cook for 5 to 7 minutes more. Repeat the process for 40 to 45 minutes, or until the ribs are pull-apart tender.

Transfer the ribs to a cutting board and let them rest, covered loosely with aluminum foil, for 10 to 15 minutes. Cut the ribs into individual pieces and serve.

NT SQUAT WITH YER SPURS ON

Ol' Kentuck
Grilled Mutton Ribs

Serves 2 to 4

Back in the 1940s, Ol' Kentuck was a popular barbecue and bootleg liquor joint on Kansas City's east side. Thus far, the origin and names of the original proprietors are unknown. We daresay the proprietors came from Kentucky and brought the Kentucky style of barbecue mutton with them. This recipe gives you a good idea of what you'll enjoy in Owensboro, Kentucky, the Barbecue Mutton Capital of the World. Ol' Kentuck was purchased by George Gates in 1946, and became the foundation for the famous Gates Bar-B-Q chain. As noted in the introduction to this chapter, Gates is one of the few barbecue joints in Kansas City where you can get barbecued mutton. The version here is not like that served at Gates.

RUB

2 tablespoons salt

2 tablespoons finely ground black pepper

1 teaspoon cayenne

RIBS

2 slabs mutton breast ribs

MOP

1 cup apple cider vinegar

⅓ cup beef or chicken stock

¼ cup canola oil

¼ cup Worcestershire sauce

1 tablespoon crushed red pepper

2 teaspoons coarse kosher salt

1 teaspoon freshly ground black pepper

Heat a cooker to medium to medium-high.

Combine all the ingredients for the rub in a small bowl and blend well. Season the ribs all over with the rub.

Combine all the ingredients for the mop in a small saucepan and heat over medium heat for about 15 minutes. Set aside.

Oil the grate and place the ribs on it bone side down. Cover and cook for 5 to 7 minutes, then mop and turn the ribs. Repeat the process for 30 to 45 minutes, or until the ribs are pull-apart tender.

Transfer the ribs to a cutting board and let them rest, covered loosely with aluminum foil, for 10 to 15 minutes. Cut the ribs into individual pieces and serve.

CHAPTER 5:

Sides

SIDES

The development of the railroad industry to move people, goods, and services over long and short distances had a major impact on the lives and culture in America and other countries. While many people today take trains for granted, many others have a passion for riding trains, learning railroad history, and collecting train memorabilia. Our friend and barbecue aficionado Bob Carruthers was one of those people. He knew a lot about trains in Australia and in America, and he rode every passenger train, several many times, in both countries.

Bob's most recent interest was the Harvey House phenomenon. Fred Harvey migrated from England to America as a teen with $10 in his pocket, got odd jobs, learned a lot, and eventually revolutionized the railroad food-service industry. Bob had plans to visit the Harvey Girls Museum in Leavenworth, Kansas, plus several sites of historical interest and research in Topeka, Kansas, but unfortunately didn't get to follow through. Suffering from a malignant brain tumor, Bob instead hopped on a train that was Bound for Glory.

At the dozens of Harvey House lunchrooms and restaurants throughout the middle and southwestern United States, travelers could get good food at a good price served by lovely, upstanding young ladies in a civilized setting. A lot has been written on the Harvey Houses, but of course our favorite is George H. Foster and Peter C. Weiglin's *The Harvey House Cookbook: Memories of Dining Along the Santa Fe Railroad*. It's interesting to see some of the sides that were in fashion in the Harvey heyday—many of them around today in some form or another. There's even an early recipe for grilled corn on the cob called "Roasting Ears" by Nelle Smith. We prefer our modern take here—but then, everything is better with bacon! Most of the sides in this chapter are for classics that have stood the test of time and won the popularity vote at many a barbecue, and perhaps even a contest or two. While we've added a few modern touches here and there, we think each one would be agreeable to Bob Carruthers, Fred Harvey, and you.

Riblicious Potato Salad

Serves 8 to 10

Potato salads have been standard fare at summer picnics, church potlucks, and family reunions for generations. The combo of colors and flavors in this recipe pleases the eyes and the palate and makes a nice complement to ribs.

2½ pounds red potatoes, diced

1 teaspoon salt, plus more for seasoning

2 large eggs

1 small yellow onion, minced

2 celery stalks, diced

1 red bell pepper, seeded and diced

¼ cup sweet or dill pickle relish

¾ cup mayonnaise

1 tablespoon prepared mustard

1 teaspoon white cane sugar

Freshly ground black pepper

Fill a large pot with water and a teaspoon of salt and bring to a boil. Add the potatoes and cook over medium heat for about 15 minutes, until tender but still firm. Drain the potatoes and transfer them to a large bowl to cool.

Put the eggs in a medium pot, cover with cold water, and bring to a boil over medium heat. Turn off the heat, cover the pot, and leave the eggs in the hot water for 15 minutes. Drain and peel the eggs under cold running water, then chop them.

Add the eggs, onion, celery, red bell pepper, pickle relish, mayonnaise, mustard, and sugar to the potatoes and stir to combine. Season with salt and pepper to taste.

Chill the salad, covered, in the refrigerator for at least 3 hours and up to overnight before serving.

Otto's Hot German Potato Salad

Serves 8 to 10

America owes a lot to southern butchers of German and Czech descent. They transformed ribs from undesirable to irresistible and made them one of the most popular restaurant and backyard foods. That's why we named this recipe for the many Ottos among male Germans in the early part of the twentieth century. We are partial to the sweet-and-sour flavor with bacon and onion accents that this salad brings to the table, and it complements any barbecue dinner, especially a rib dinner.

3½ pounds medium Idaho russet potatoes

1 teaspoon salt, plus more for boiling the potatoes

3 beef bouillon cubes

⅓ cup warm water, or more as needed

12 thick slices bacon

1 large sweet onion, diced

½ cup apple cider vinegar

1 teaspoon freshly ground black pepper

3 tablespoons white cane sugar

Place the potatoes in a large pot and cover them with water. Add some salt and bring to a boil over medium heat. Cook until fork-tender, about 20 minutes. Drain and set aside to cool, then peel and cut into small chunks.

Dissolve the bouillon cubes in ⅓ cup of warm water; set aside. Fry the bacon in a large stainless-steel skillet over medium heat until crisp. Transfer to a paper towel to drain and add the onion to the bacon grease. Sauté the onion over medium heat until soft, 3 to 4 minutes. Add the vinegar, 1 teaspoon of salt, the pepper, sugar, and bouillon. Bring to a boil over medium heat, then add the potatoes and simmer for 4 minutes. Add the crispy bacon and toss the ingredients until the potatoes are coated. Add a small amount of water if you like a thinner consistency. Serve warm.

Spring Greens Salad with Cheese and Tomato

Serves 10 to 12

Thank goodness spring greens, also called field greens, are available at any time of year. The best, of course, are the fresh salad greens from your own spring garden, a farmers' market, or a community-supported agriculture vendor. When you can't get fresh and local, however, you'll find good spring salad greens in most supermarket produce sections. This combo of spring greens, cheese and tomatoes, is easy, light, and a special hit with guests who feel guilty about how many ribs they are eating.

4 cups assorted spring salad greens

4 medium tomatoes, sliced

2 ripe avocados, peeled, pitted, and sliced

1 to 2 cups crumbled low-fat feta or fresh mozzarella cheese cut into small chunks

½ teaspoon crushed dried marjoram

½ teaspoon crushed dried dill

½ teaspoon crushed dried oregano

½ cup red wine vinegar

½ cup olive oil

1 teaspoon Dijon mustard

2 large cloves garlic, pressed

Salt and freshly ground black pepper

Place the lettuce, tomatoes, avocados, and cheese in a large bowl and toss to mix.

Place the marjoram, dill, and oregano in a lidded jar or cruet. Add the vinegar and shake to mix. Add the olive oil, mustard, and garlic and shake well. Just before serving, pour the vinaigrette over the salad and toss, then add salt and pepper to taste.

Hush Puppies

Serves 8 to 10

In Carolina barbecue and fish joints you'll be served hush puppies without having to ask. We wouldn't mind seeing that tradition spread across America. Theirs are usually in the shape of large capsules. Ours in this recipe are balls. We like to start with this basic recipe, but there are many variations. Texans or New Mexicans would likely add a tablespoon of chopped jalapeño or chopped fire-roasted Hatch chiles. If you've never enjoyed hush puppies with ribs, you're in for a treat!

2 cups self-rising white
    cornmeal (see Note)

¾ cup self-rising flour

½ teaspoon salt

½ teaspoon black pepper

1 medium yellow onion, minced or grated

2 large eggs

1 to 1½ cups buttermilk, as desired

Vegetable oil, peanut oil, or
    pure lard for deep-frying

Mix the cornmeal, flour, salt, pepper, onion, and eggs in a large bowl. Slowly add buttermilk and stir until the mixture isn't runny when you take a scoop. We prefer a thick batter. If you like it thin, mix in more buttermilk.

Heat the oil in a large deep pot over medium-high heat until it reaches 350°F on a deep-frying thermometer. Use a small ice cream or butter scoop and drop scoops of batter into the oil. When the balls rise to the top, gently turn them with a slotted spoon. Cook for about 3 to 5 minutes total, until they are golden or light brown. Drain on paper towels before serving in a basket or bowl.

Note: You also can use 1 cup of self-rising white cornmeal and 1 cup of self-rising yellow cornmeal.

Southern Ladies Corn Bread

Serves 6 to 8

Sweet or not? Southern ladies—and gentlemen, as well—will never agree on which corn bread is best. That's why sugar is optional in this recipe. If you are serving your ribs with a sweet sauce, omit the sugar in this recipe. With naked or sour-sauced ribs, serve sweet corn bread.

¾ cup yellow cornmeal

¼ cup all-purpose flour

2 tablespoons white cane sugar (optional)

1 teaspoon salt

1 teaspoon baking powder

½ teaspoon baking soda

1 large egg

1 cup whole milk

½ cup buttermilk

3 tablespoons unsalted butter

Combine the cornmeal, flour, sugar (if using), salt, baking powder, and baking soda in a large bowl and stir to blend.

In a separate bowl, lightly beat the egg. Add ½ cup of the milk and whisk until mixed, then add the buttermilk and whisk until mixed.

Preheat the oven to 350°F.

Melt the butter in a medium cast-iron skillet over medium heat. Pour the liquid ingredients over the dry ingredients in the bowl. Pour the corn bread mixture into the skillet, then add the remaining milk without stirring. Bake for 25 minutes. Serve warm.

REBIRTH OF THE SANDWICH

by Mason Steinberg, former proprietor of Old Mill BBQ, Omaha, Nebraska

In 1949, I was working for my family at Cornhusker Packing Company in South Omaha, next to the world's largest livestock market. Back in those days, Omaha had about twenty-seven animal-slaughter packing facilities.

One hot, humid afternoon, my uncle Leo called me into the office and told me to give four employees who were working in the hide cellar a ride to All Nations, a three-story flophouse where packinghouse employees lived and paid their rent by the day. We always could find someone to work, as we would pay spot labor cash for the day.

That was the day I first smelled the smoke!

That not-very-picturesque neighborhood had a couple of cheap restaurants and, of course, a bar on the corner. The area of 25th and Q Street had been known as "Bloody Corner" since Prohibition Days. It was an area that the police would leave alone unless they were looking for someone special, such as a suspect, or at least a lead on where to find a suspect. Bloody Corner also was just east of the center of male social life in South Omaha, Light'n Johnson's "7th Ward Club." The head of our hide crew, "Money Man," lent money and was well thought of—at least to his face. He didn't care what the money was for—gambling, barbecue, women, you name it. Money Man and Light'n made sure that my friends and I were safe. We only went there for barbecue late on Friday or Saturday nights after ball games.

Just north of the Bloody Corner bar you could smell the aroma and see smoke com'n out of a little white building housing a barbecue restaurant called the Silver Pit BBQ on the other side of All Nations, near an empty lot for parking and storefront businesses catering to the neighborhood types. On weekends and Mondays, when the cowboys came to town with trucks of cattle, the area was a wide-open circus, with drunks, barbecue, fights, and girls.

You get the picture?

It took me about a month to get up enough nerve to go into this wonderful-smelling building, and there I met Jasper Jones. The restaurant remains to this day the citadel of early barbecue in Omaha.

A screen door would hit you in the butt if you weren't fast enough when entering. To the left was an old soft drink machine, with one narrow vertical door where you could pull out your drink for the cost of a dime—any flavor of Whistle. There were two rooms, seating for maybe twenty people, and it was clean, with whitewashed walls. Straight in front was the counter with a chalkboard menu and a short, balding, slightly heavyset

black man named Jasper Jones behind it. He would just look at you, waiting for you to order or ask a question, and then he would speak.

I was in strange territory, a nervous fifteen-year-old white kid out of his element. There I saw on the menu a rib sandwich. I didn't even know what a rib sandwich was—beef, pork, how many bones, how was it served? "Rib sandwich," I blurted out. Mild, medium, hot sauce on the side, was my next decision. "Hot." Mr. Jones looked up at me and replied, "I'll let you know when you can have my hot sauce, boy." "Mild," I said. After that rib sandwich, I was still hungry. I ordered a beef brisket sandwich, "Medium." I got it! It was smoky flavored, warm, fresh out of the pit, and I could taste the rub and hickory smoke that was used to enhance the underlying beef flavor. Later, Jasper told me a good rub can be used for beef, pork, chicken, fish, goat, coon, possum, beaver, or anything else.

I was addicted from that first day, and I've never wanted to go through rehab.

About six weeks after that, the boy became a barbecue man and was given the hot sauce! There were many times my cousin Irv and I would eat at the Silver Pit three or four days a week.

It was rumored that John Montagu, Lord Sandwich, was a persistent gambler and didn't have time for formal eating. Just two slices of bread with meat in the middle is how it began with him. The beginning of what we know today as a sandwich. People in the area near the Silver Pit BBQ had very little time for lunch. Maybe Jasper was on to something, too. Lord Sandwich would have rolled over in his grave if he saw the barbecue rib sandwich. Four cooked-to-perfection pork spareribs (not overcooked and falling off the bone, as so many are today) were sandwiched between two slices of barbecue bread, with sauce on the side. When you bit into the meat, it would pull away from the bone easily, leaving the rest of the meat in place. (In case you're wondering, "barbecue bread" is square white bread—how barbecue was served for maybe the last seventy-five to a hundred years).

Jasper and I became great friends. Actually he was my mentor for about four years until I went away to college.

In 1991, when I opened Old Mill BBQ in Omaha, Nebraska, I featured a Rib Sandwich, four succulent spareribs between two slices of day-old barbecue bread. The bread is better if it's a day old. If it's too fresh, it sticks to your teeth and roof of your mouth. I don't recall ever seeing two slices of barbecue bread with four rib bones in the middle anyplace else.

I might eat one slice while consuming the ribs and then use the other piece for dessert. Just add some sauce to half the slice and fold over. Now that's a dessert fit for a king—or should I say a lord!

Heartland Grilled Corn on the Cob

Serves 12

This recipe honors the abundance of America's sweet and field corn that comes from the heartland. There's something about the heartland *terroir* that makes corn and other fresh produce absolutely delicious! Although field corn is grown primarily for livestock feed, ethanol, or adult beverages, when it is grilled we've enjoyed field corn as much as sweet. This recipe delivers a combination of sweetness, spice, and smoke that your guests will devour with as much gusto as the ribs.

12 ears corn on the cob, with husks

¼ cup barbecue rub

2 tablespoons freshly ground black pepper

12 thin slices lean bacon

Remove and discard any dry outer corn husks. Pull the husks down, but don't remove them. Hold the corn under cold running water while removing the corn silk.

Heat a grill to medium to medium-high.

Pat the corn dry with paper towels and sprinkle it with the rub and pepper. Wrap the corn in bacon and pull the husks over it. Wrap each ear in a 12-inch square of aluminum foil. Grill for about 15 minutes over direct heat, turning frequently.

Remove the corn from the grill and leave it in the foil for 20 minutes before serving.

RIBS IN HONEYSUCKLE ROSE II

by Ardie A. Davis

In 1994, I was invited to judge ribs with the late Don "Doc" Gillis and Joe Phelps—cofounders of the *National Barbecue News*—at the Great American Rib Cook-Off over Memorial Day weekend in Cleveland, Ohio. The featured entertainer to close out the event that year was Willie Nelson and his band. As longtime admirers of Willie's music, we managed to get front-row seats. We had asked (begged!) the event organizers to see if they could get us an audience with Willie after the concert. When we were told it was arranged, Don, Joe, and I

Pineapple Coleslaw

Serves 6 to 8

The sweet-and-sour flavor combo in this slaw goes well with sweet ribs, sour ribs, or naked ribs. And making it couldn't be easier.

1 cup mayonnaise

½ cane white cane sugar

3 tablespoons apple cider vinegar

1 (8-ounce) can pineapple chunks, drained and chunks cut in half

1 (1-pound) bag coleslaw mix, angel hair or traditional

Combine the mayonnaise, sugar, and vinegar in a small bowl and whisk to blend. Place the pineapple chunks and coleslaw mix in a large bowl and toss to combine. Pour the dressing over the coleslaw mixture and toss to coat. Chill for at least 2 hours and up to overnight before serving.

were as excited as kids in summer when the ice cream truck arrives in the neighborhood.

After the concert we waited outside Willie's tour bus, Honeysuckle Rose II. Prior to that, we had taken up a collection of ribs from contestants and arranged to have them delivered to Willie. Maybe that's why it was so long before we were invited on the bus! We didn't mind, as it was a chance of a lifetime that we would have waited all night for. When the bus door opened and we climbed aboard, Willie gave us a friendly welcome, thanked us for the ribs, and asked us to sit down for a visit. We knew the ribs had been appreciated, as all we saw in the kitchen was a plate of clean rib bones. He said he liked them, and we knew he was telling the truth.

Willie was kind enough to pose with us for some photos before we sat down to visit. Doc and Joe told Willie how much we've appreciated his music over the years, and what a great concert it was, and how honored we were to meet him in person. We talked about barbecue, country music, and exchanged a few stories. When my turn came up, I shared a true story about a Kansas lady I know who is one of his greatest fans. She likes Willie so much that every time her husband made love to her, she required him to wear the bandana she had caught when Willie tossed it into the audience at a Kansas State Fair concert. "He died of a heart attack," I said. Laughter burst out and Willie said, "Well, at least he died with a smile on his face."

Asian Coleslaw

Serves 6 to 8

This slaw with an Asian accent delivers sweet and sour with crunch. It matches well with any style of ribs.

SALAD

1 head Napa cabbage, shredded

**5 scallions, both white and
  green parts, thinly sliced**

DRESSING

1 cup white cane sugar

½ cup rice vinegar

1 tablespoon soy sauce

½ cup canola oil

TOPPINGS

**1 (3-ounce) package ramen
  noodles, crushed**

1 2.25-ounce package sliced almonds

½ cup sunflower seeds

Preheat the oven to 300°F.

In a large bowl, combine the cabbage and scallions and toss to mix.

To make the dressing, combine the sugar, vinegar, and soy sauce in a medium saucepan and heat over low heat until the sugar dissolves. Cool, then whisk in the canola oil.

Place the ramen noodles, almonds, and sunflower seeds on a baking sheet and bake for 5 to 10 minutes, or until toasted, stirring often and watching carefully.

Pour the dressing over the cabbage mixture and toss to coat. Just before serving, sprinkle the toasted mixture over the salad and toss well.

Slow-Cooked Baked Beans

Serves 25 to 30

There are many ways to prepare delicious beans for a rib feast. This is one of the easiest, and it doesn't sacrifice flavor for convenience. If, for some reason, you have rib meat left over, you can chop it up and add it to your beans. You also could use your cooked trimmings from St. Louis–style ribs (see page 24).

2 (15-ounce) cans great northern
   beans, drained and rinsed

1 cup firmly packed dark brown sugar

¾ cup molasses

2 tablespoons sweet barbecue sauce

2 tablespoons ketchup

1 (7-pound) can baked beans,
   drained and rinsed

1 (15-ounce) can pork and
   beans, drained and rinsed

1½ cups chopped cooked rib meat

Place all the ingredients in a slow cooker, turn to high, and cook until boiling, about 2 hours. Reduce the heat to low and cook for at least 6 hours and up to overnight.

Mom's Homemade Baked Beans

Serves 10 to 12

The Baron has enjoyed these beans for as long as he can remember. Mary Kirk, Paul's mother, has prepared this dish for family feasts for more than half a century, and no one has tired of it yet. In fact, they can't wait for the next family feast!

1 pound dried navy or great
  northern beans

½ cup firmly packed dark brown sugar

⅓ cup sorghum or molasses

1 tablespoon soy sauce

1 teaspoon Worcestershire sauce

½ teaspoon dry mustard

½ teaspoon salt

½ medium yellow onion, diced

¼ to ½ pound bacon square
  (smoked hog jowl), diced

Wash and pick through the beans, then place them in a large bowl and cover with cold water. Soak overnight, adding more water if necessary.

Drain and rinse the beans. Put them in a saucepan, cover with fresh water, and bring to a boil over medium heat. Boil until soft, then drain, reserving the broth.

Preheat the oven to 275°F.

In a small bowl, combine the brown sugar, sorghum, soy sauce, Worcestershire sauce, mustard, and salt and whisk to blend. Layer the beans, onion, diced bacon, and brown sugar mixture in a bean pot or ovenproof dish. Add the reserved bean broth to the beans until you reach your desired consistency.

Bake uncovered for 5 to 8 hours, stirring occasionally. If the beans seem to be getting too brown, cover the dish.

Macaroni Salad

Serves 12 to 16

Along with barbecue beans, a favorite at family feasts and get-togethers with friends is a classic macaroni salad. This one is easy to make and rich with color, and it complements any style of ribs.

4 cups elbow macaroni, cooked until still a little firm and rinsed with cold water

½ large red onion, diced

1 yellow or orange bell pepper, seeded and diced

10 to 12 radishes, chopped

1 (12-ounce) package frozen peas, thawed

1 cup mayonnaise

Salt and freshly ground black pepper

1 cup shredded cheddar cheese

Combine the macaroni, onion, bell pepper, radishes, and peas in a large salad bowl. Stir in the mayonnaise and add salt and pepper to taste. Stir in the shredded cheese. Chill for 1 to 2 hours before serving.

Fruit Salad with Mint

Serves 10 to 12

Serve this light and healthy salad to guests who need a guilt exemption for all the ribs they are eating. With this complementary side of fresh fruit, they can tell themselves, "But I also ate a lot of fruit salad with my ribs," and they will like this salad so much that their self-reassurance will be true.

1 cantaloupe, peeled, seeded, and cubed

1 honeydew melon, peeled, seeded, and cubed

4 kiwi fruits, peeled and sliced

1 quart strawberries, hulled and halved

1 pint fresh blueberries

¼ cup clover or other mild-flavored honey

1 cup fresh orange juice

3 sprigs fresh mint

Place the fruit in a large serving bowl. Combine the honey and orange juice in a small bowl and whisk to blend. Add the mint sprigs to the salad (don't chop them), pour the dressing over the top, and toss gently to mix. Chill for 4 or more hours, then remove the mint before serving.

Note: Other fresh fruit can be added to your liking. We don't recommend bananas, since they turn brown.

MAY THE WORST RIBS WIN!
John Willingham's Legendary Victory in Cleveland

by Phil Litman, foodie and expert barbecue judge

John Willingham, legendary pitmaster, restaurateur, cookbook author, and inventor of the W'ham Turbo Cooker, arrived in Cleveland, Ohio, for the Great American Rib Cook-Off and Music Festival with his trailer and crew quite late due to several mechanical and tire problems he experienced on the way from his hometown of Memphis, Tennessee. I was fortunate to be selected as one of the certified judges in the cook-off's regular panel.

I met John as he pulled in and got his assigned vendor spot. He learned from the official meat purveyor for the contest that, because he was so late, all the cases of pork loin baby back ribs were already sold or spoken for by other vendors, and the best he could do were St. Louis–cut ribs. The baby backs were what the crowds preferred. John told the meat purveyor that instead of the St. Louis–cut ribs he wanted nothing but the cheapest junk ribs available, period! He told me, "I`ll show them. . . . I`m going to outsell all the competing rib vendors and win the sanctioned contest, and the People's Choice Award, too." I was there to bear witness that John Willingham did all

Cheese Garlic Bread

Makes about 24 slices

When Paul's family gathers, Paul gets to make the garlic bread. One of his sisters used to make the garlic bread, and Paul would ask, "How much garlic did you use?" Paul loves garlic, so he wanted to make sure the bread was loaded with it. His sister got tired of his complaints about not enough garlic, so she gave him the task of making the garlic bread from then on. This one is full of garlic flavor, it's easy, and it can even be made ahead and frozen. We recommend making three loaves and freezing the other two for future meals.

1 loaf French bread

8 tablespoons (1 stick) unsalted butter, softened

3 to 5 large cloves garlic, pressed

1 teaspoon crushed dried parsley

⅓ cup freshly grated Parmesan cheese

Preheat the oven to 375°F.

Cut the bread into 1-inch-thick slices, but don't cut all the way through. Combine the butter, garlic, parsley, and Parmesan cheese in a medium bowl and mix thoroughly. Spread the mixture in between slices and on top of each slice of bread. Wrap the loaf in heavy-duty aluminum foil, leaving the top open down the middle, and bake for 15 minutes, or until heated through.

three! John always swore before that event, during it, and to this very day, that there's "No brag . . . just fact!" to his barbecue success. In my opinion, John not only is a great southern gentleman, but also the undisputed heavyweight barbecue champion of the world.

Since I first met John and his wife, Marge, in 1985 at the Memphis in May World Championship Barbecue Cooking Contest at Tom Lee Park in Memphis, Tennessee, my late wife Cheryl and I found him to be a tough competitor and at the same time always friendly, outgoing, and gracious.

Tomato Bread

Makes 2 loaves

White sandwich bread, also called "bunny bread," is what you can expect at most rib joints in America. We like it for sopping up grease and sauce to set aside for eating at the end of our meal if we don't fill up on ribs. At home you can crank up the quality of your rib bread with this incredibly flavorful combo of fennel, rosemary, oregano, basil, and garlic. Instead of using it for sopping, stuff rib meat pulled from the bones between two slices of tomato bread and enjoy a unique gourmet rib sandwich.

2 cups tomato juice

½ cup tomato sauce

2 tablespoons unsalted butter

6 to 6½ cups all-purpose flour, plus more for kneading

2 tablespoons active dry yeast

3 tablespoons white cane sugar

1 teaspoon salt

½ teaspoon dried basil

¾ teaspoon crushed dried oregano

¼ teaspoon ground rosemary

¼ teaspoon ground fennel

2 large cloves garlic, pressed

Butter a large bowl and two 9-inch loaf pans and set them aside.

Combine the tomato juice, tomato sauce, and butter in a medium saucepan over low heat and warm it to lukewarm.

In a large mixer bowl, combine 3 cups of the flour with the yeast, sugar, salt, basil, oregano, rosemary, and fennel. Add the warmed tomato mixture and the garlic. Mix with the dough hook on medium speed for 3 minutes (or by hand with 300 strokes), scraping the bowl frequently. Slowly and gradually add 3 to 3½ cups more flour, until the dough is firm enough to handle, not sticky. Turn out the dough onto a floured surface and knead until it is smooth and elastic, adding more flour as necessary.

Place the dough in the buttered bowl, cover, and let rise in a warm place until doubled, about 1 hour. Punch down, then let rest for 15 minutes.

Shape the dough into two loaves and place each in a prepared pan. Cover loosely and let rise until nearly doubled, about 45 minutes.

Preheat the oven to 375°F. Bake the loaves for 10 minutes, then reduce the heat to 350°F and bake for 30 minutes more, or until the loaves sound hollow when tapped. Remove the bread from the pans and cool on a wire rack before slicing and serving.

Note: A rib sandwich with this bread is delicious!

WHAT'S A RIB SANDWICH, AND HOW DO YOU EAT IT?

We'll never forget our first rib sandwich. What shocked us was that the rib meat in the sandwich was still on the bones. Was this a joke, or what? It was not. The rib sandwich origin stories we've heard thus far are heavy on speculation and light on documentation. We hope someone will step forth with the true story, but thus far we're still waiting.

The traditional rib sandwich features at least four sparerib bones atop a slice of white bread, with sauce on the ribs or to the side and another slice of white bread to the side. Eating a rib sandwich is much the same as eating ribs the way you always do. You pick them up, pull the bone apart if it isn't already sliced, and eat a rib at a time. The added bonus of a rib sandwich is bread to sop up sauce and grease—although many rib joints today serve ribs with bread on the side or with multiple bread slices atop the slab anyway.

Of course, when most people think of a rib sandwich they picture McDonald's popular version of a rib sandwich, the McRib. It is boneless cooked pork meat shaped like a portion of loin slab, served in a hoagie roll with barbecue sauce, pickles, and onion. Paul likes them. Ardie would rather eat the Angus Burger. When Ardie administers the Judges' Oath at barbecue contests, he begins with, "If you can taste the difference between a McRib sandwich and real barbecue, please stand, raise your right hand, and repeat after me, 'I do solemnly swear. . . .'"

CHAPTER 6:
Desserts

HOMEMADE DESSERTS

We don't know who coined the popular expression "Life is short. Eat dessert first." We do know it hasn't taken hold. Dessert has been and is to this day always served last. You've devoured the ribs and sides. Now it's time for some sweetness, the end of a glorious feast.

Our friend Bob Carruthers liked barbecue ribs, Krystal burgers, Iron Kettle whiskey burgers, fries, Tater Tots, barbecue beans, salads, and many other sides. He also liked desserts. Truth be known, Bob's favorite category at The Jack was dessert. After several hours of judging some of the world's best barbecue at the Jack Daniel's World Championship Invitational Barbecue, Bob always saved room for judging the creative sweet wonders visited upon the judges.

Many competition barbecuers have caught on to sweetness as the X-factor in winning a contest in other categories, too—so much that some judges, when faced with contest boxes full of sugar-glazed ribs, have quipped, "Isn't the dessert category supposed to be last?" The desserts in this chapter are the perfect finale to complement a feast of ribs. A few are from our childhood, many others are regional favorites from our years of barbecue travels, and we hope they all become favorites at your rib dinners!

Each feast must end. These sweet endings are for you, Bob, and all the other dessert lovers out there.

Grandma LeCluyse's Peach Cobbler

Serves 8 to 10

One of the most popular and easy-to-make desserts at any barbecue is the cobbler. You can make any kind you want—peach, blackberry, blueberry, strawberry, or rhubarb, for starters. Topped with homemade or store-bought vanilla ice cream, it just doesn't get any better. This is the peach cobbler Paul grew up with, compliments of his grandma LeCluyse. She used lard in the crust, and while we prefer it that way, you can use butter or shortening, if you like.

8 large ripe peaches, peeled, pitted, and sliced

1 cup white cane sugar

½ teaspoon ground cinnamon

⅛ teaspoon freshly grated nutmeg

3½ cups all-purpose flour

¾ cup lard, butter, or shortening

1 large egg, lightly beaten

1 tablespoon apple cider vinegar

½ cup ice water

6 tablespoons (¾ stick) unsalted butter

Vanilla ice cream (recipe follows), for serving

Preheat the oven to 350°F.

Place the peaches in a large bowl, add the sugar, cinnamon, and nutmeg, and mix thoroughly. Set aside.

Use a pastry cutter, two forks, or your hands to mix the flour and lard together until the mixture is well-combined and crumbly. Add the egg, vinegar, and ice water and stir until the dough comes together, but don't overwork it. Form the dough into a ball, transfer it to a floured surface, and gently shape it into a rectangle. Roll out the dough into a rectangle large enough to fit in the bottom and up the sides of a 9 by 13-inch baking dish. Carefully transfer the dough to the baking dish, draping it over the floured rolling pin if necessary, and press it in. Pour in the peach mixture. Dot the top of the mixture with the tablespoons of butter. Bake for 55 minutes, or until the filling is bubbly and the crust is golden brown.

Top with vanilla ice cream and enjoy.

Vanilla Ice Cream

Makes about 4 quarts, serving 10 to 12

Paul's father used to make this when his family had barbecues. It was great on top of Grandma LeCluyse's cobblers. And, yes, they all got to take turns cranking the ice cream, as this was before the electric home freezers.

4 large eggs

2 cups white cane sugar

1 (14-ounce) can sweetened condensed milk

1 (12-ounce) can evaporated milk

¼ teaspoon sea salt

2 tablespoons vanilla extract

½ gallon whole milk or as needed to top off your freezer can

In a large bowl, beat the eggs well. Add the sugar, sweetened condensed milk, evaporated milk, sea salt, and vanilla and beat well. Pour the mixture into the freezer can of your ice cream maker and add milk (and/or fruit, if desired) until the mixture is 2 to 4 inches from the top.

Secure the lid and process according to your manufacturer's directions. Remove the ice cream from the container and freeze to the desired firmness.

Note: You can add up to 4 cups chopped sweetened fruit of your choice along with or instead of the whole milk to make fruit ice cream, instead.

EVERYONE LOVES FREE RIBS!

by Guy Simpson, Kansas City Rib Doctor

Back in 1986, the Kansas City Barbecue Society was asked to cook barbecue for the Vietnam veterans who held their national convention in Kansas City, Missouri, at Crown Center. The Barbecue Society jumped at the challenge, including Donna and Ted McClure's Pretty Damn Tasty team, the Master Basters, Gary and Carolyn Wells, KC Baron of Barbecue Paul Kirk, Janeyce Michel-Cupito and Bill Cupito of the Powder Puff team, and, of course, the Kansas City Rib Doctor. We had our pits ready to go, and as the late Paul Harvey used to say, "Here's the rest of the story."

One of our members, whom we won't identify, volunteered to call around and get a good price for us, since we were donating the ribs and our services. He called around and got us a great price—$.99 a pound for pork ribs.

When we got the ribs, we discovered a problem. They looked like they were straight out of a Fred Flintstone adventure. They were the

Blackberry Cobbler

Serves 6 to 8

British immigrants are credited with bringing the cobbler concept to America. Cobblers became especially popular in the South, where you'll find them everywhere.

2 cups fresh blackberries

1 cup water

⅔ cup white cane sugar

2 tablespoons all-purpose flour, plus more for rolling

2 cups store-bought biscuit mix

½ to ¾ cup milk

2 tablespoons cold unsalted butter, cut into small pieces

Vanilla ice cream (recipe precedes), for serving

Preheat the oven to 450°F. Butter a 2-quart baking dish.

Combine the blackberries, water, sugar, and 1 tablespoon flour in a medium saucepan over medium heat. Bring to a boil, then reduce the heat and simmer for 3 to 5 minutes. Remove from the heat and set aside.

Place the biscuit mix in a large bowl and stir in enough milk to make a soft, slightly sticky dough. Turn out the dough on a floured surface and pat and roll it into a square large enough to fit the baking dish.

Cut the dough into 1-inch-wide strips. Pour about 1 cup of the blackberry mixture into the bottom of the prepared baking dish. Arrange half of the dough strips on top, placing them about ½ inch apart. Dot the top with half the butter. Bake until the crust is brown, 8 to 12 minutes, then remove from the oven and pour the remaining berry mixture over the top. Arrange the other half of the dough strips on top running the other direction, dot with the remaining butter, and bake for 8 to 12 minutes longer, or until the crust is brown. Serve warm with ice cream.

size of the brontosaurus ribs that tipped over Fred's vehicle. All of the slabs were more than 7 pounds, and the largest was 8¼ pounds (the standard then was 2½ to 3 pounds). The fat pockets between the big bones were sooooo big that when we cooked them, the pockets disappeared and left big holes in the ribs so they looked like Dirty Harry had shot them with his .44 Magnum! It might have been the powder burns that gave it away.

We doctored the not-so-pretty ribs with a lot of barbecue sauce and served them. The strangest part is that a lot of the veterans came over to the pits and complimented us on the great barbecue that they had just eaten. We were amazed at how free smoked ribs cooked Kansas City style could be such a big hit—no matter what we started with!

Caramel Crisp Rice Cereal Bars

Makes 32 bars, depending on how large you want them

One of our favorite childhood desserts was Rice Krispies treats. Now we have an even better version from Paul's friend Joyce, who serves these for dessert with her barbecue ribs feasts. They are a great sweet finish to a barbecue.

CRISP RICE CEREAL MIX

½ pound (2 sticks) unsalted butter

2 (10-ounce) packages large marshmallows

12 cups crisp rice cereal (about one 18-ounce box)

CARAMEL MIXTURE

1 (14-ounce) package caramels

1 (14-ounce) can sweetened condensed milk

8 tablespoons (1 stick) unsalted butter

Butter a 10 by 15-inch rimmed baking sheet and set it aside.

For the cereal mix, place 1 stick of the butter in a very large microwave-safe bowl and microwave until melted, about 1 minute. Stir in 1 package of the marshmallows, then microwave until the marshmallows begin to melt, about 2 minutes. Stir together the butter and marshmallows, then stir in 6 cups of the cereal until evenly coated. Pour the mixture into the prepared baking pan and pat it into an even layer. Allow it to cool, then turn it out onto a large sheet of wax paper. Clean and butter the baking sheet, then repeat with the remaining butter, marshmallows, and cereal.

Combine the caramels, sweetened condensed milk, and butter in a medium saucepan over medium-low heat and stir often until melted together. Pour the mixture on top of one rectangle of cereal, spread it evenly, then put the other cereal rectangle on top. Allow to cool, then cut into squares.

Southern Sweet Potato Pie

Serves 8

In our travels, we've enjoyed many a piece of sweet potato pie, or "potato pie" as it's often called, in the South. Here's an easy and delicious version we like.

2½ cups mashed cooked sweet potatoes (2 to 3 medium potatoes)

¾ cup white cane sugar

½ cup firmly packed light brown sugar

1 (3.4-ounce) package vanilla instant pudding

¾ cup evaporated milk

2 large eggs

6 tablespoons (¾ stick) unsalted butter, at room temperature

1 tablespoon vanilla extract

1½ teaspoons ground cinnamon

¼ teaspoon freshly grated nutmeg

1 (9-inch) unbaked pie shell

Preheat the oven to 450°F.

Combine the sweet potatoes, sugars, pudding mix, evaporated milk, eggs, butter, vanilla, cinnamon, and nutmeg in a large bowl and mix until well blended. Spread evenly into the unbaked pie shell.

Bake for 10 minutes. Reduce the oven temperature to 350°F and bake until set in the middle, about 40 minutes more.

Cool completely on a wire rack before cutting and serving.

Old-Fashioned Banana Pudding

Serves 6 to 8

This is another popular dessert we have found in many Carolina homes and restaurants. It's a mellow, creamy, cool, and refreshing finish to a feast of tangy, spicy ribs.

1 cup white cane sugar

3 large eggs, beaten

Pinch of sea salt

2 tablespoons cornstarch or arrowroot

2 cups whole milk or cream

1 teaspoon vanilla extract

1 (12-ounce) box vanilla wafers

3 to 4 ripe medium bananas, sliced

In a medium saucepan, lightly beat the sugar and eggs until blended. Stir in the salt, cornstarch, and milk and bring to a boil over medium-high heat, whisking constantly until thickened. Remove from the heat and stir in the vanilla.

Arrange a layer of vanilla wafers in the bottom of a serving bowl, then top with a layer of banana slices, followed by a layer of the pudding. Repeat, as desired, until all of the pudding and bananas have been used. Chill for at least 2 hours before serving.

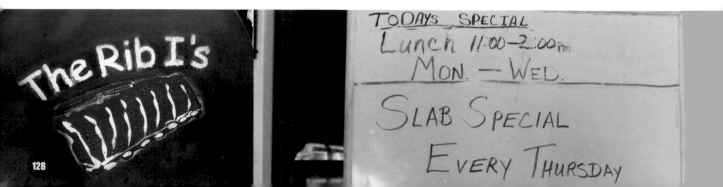

Lazy Daisy Cake

Serves 6 to 8

This is a dessert Paul grew up with at family barbecue feasts and other gatherings. When Paul's mother made it, he remembers as a small child helping her blend yellow food coloring with oleo that looked like Crisco. They would work it until it was the color of butter. We now call it margarine, but butter is better.

CAKE

2 large eggs, lightly beaten

1 cup white cane sugar

½ teaspoon sea salt

1 teaspoon vanilla extract

1 tablespoon unsalted butter, melted

½ cup whole milk, lukewarm

1 cup all-purpose flour

1 teaspoon baking powder

TOPPING

3 tablespoons unsalted butter

5 tablespoons light brown sugar

2 tablespoons cream or whole milk

½ cup shredded sweetened coconut

Preheat the oven to 350°F. Butter an 8-inch square cake pan.

In a large bowl, combine the eggs, sugar, salt, and vanilla. Add the melted butter to the lukewarm milk and beat it into the egg mixture. Add the flour and baking powder and beat just until combined.

Pour the batter into the prepared pan and bake for 35 minutes, or until a toothpick inserted in the middle comes out clean.

Set the oven to broil.

While the cake is still warm, make the topping: Heat the butter, brown sugar, and cream in a medium saucepan over low heat, stirring, until the sugar is dissolved. Stir in the coconut. Pour the topping onto the cake. Brown the topping under the broiler, watching closely so it doesn't burn.

Cool the cake on a wire rack, then slice and serve.

RIBS NEVER SAY NEVER!

by "Smoky Jon" Olson, proprietor of Smoky Jon's #1 BBQ in Madison, Wisconsin

Smoky Jon's #1 BBQ was in Minneapolis, Minnesota, at a huge national Ribfest in 1991. The event was very busy, and we were slammed with hungry rib lovers. Blues great "Kid" Jonny Lang and rock legends The Guess Who drew huge crowds to downtown Minneapolis that Friday night, and we sold just under two thousand pounds of ribs. It didn't hurt that we had famous actor-director Emilio Estevez and stunning pop icon Paula Abdul in our booth for three hours during prime-time dinner hours.

The competition cooking was going to take place on Saturday, and I discovered I had a mechanical problem with my pit. At 11:00 P.M. Friday night, I received my judging time from the promoters. I needed an electrician to check out my pit, but the electrician had gone home and wouldn't return until 9:00 A.M. Saturday—just two hours before my 11:00 A.M. judging time. There was no way I could prepare my competition ribs in two hours, so I asked the promoters for a later judging time, and they changed it to 2:00 P.M. Great!

The electrician came at 9:00 A.M. Saturday and repaired my pit, and my Hog-Heavenly Rib Delights were on their way to perfection for the 2:00 P.M. judging time—or so I thought. Our crew was getting our barbecue booth ready for the Ribfest crowds when the same promoter who had originally given me the 2:00 P.M. judging time stopped by and said, "You have to have your ribs and sauce entries ready at 11:00 A.M. for the judges or you will be disqualified," and then turned and walked—no, ran—away from our booth. I was livid!

It was 10:23 A.M., and I had to adapt, improvise, and overcome! I had thirty-seven minutes to prepare my ribs and sauce entries for the judges. This is what I did:

I had two fresh, hot charcoal grills ready for lunch. We had pulled twenty cases of ribs at midnight on Friday and cooked them overnight for our Saturday rib sales. I took thirty slabs, selecting the meatiest, most tender ribs, and I grilled those thirty slabs till they were hot, juicy, and perfectly done, then applied my competition sauce. Then I cut "Hollywood-style" ribs (a cut of a rib with meat on both sides of the bone) from eight different slabs of the thirty I had on the grill. We were closing the lid on our judging box when the judging representative arrived at 11:00 A.M. to take our rib and sauce entries to the blind judging areas.

At the awards ceremony on Sunday afternoon, we won first and third for our ribs and sauce. Never say never!

Mama Ethel's Strawberry Shortcake

Serves 8 to 10

Another dessert we really love after consuming a fair amount of barbecued ribs is strawberry shortcake. It is easy to make either from scratch or with store-bought angel food cake or even a biscuit. Although Ardie's maternal grandmother, Ethel Fitzpatrick Hamm, a.k.a. Mama Ethel, was as likely to serve her strawberry dessert with leftover baking powder biscuits or store-bought shortcake, we've named this one in her honor.

4 cups sliced fresh strawberries

⅓ cup plus ¼ cup white cane sugar

3 cups all-purpose flour

4 teaspoons baking powder

½ pound (2 sticks) unsalted butter

⅔ cup heavy cream

1 large egg, beaten

Whipped cream, for serving

Preheat the oven to 350°F.

In a large bowl, combine the strawberries and ⅓ cup of the sugar. Stir and mash them together until the strawberries release some juices, then cover and refrigerate.

In a large bowl, whisk together the flour, remaining ¼ cup sugar, and baking powder. Use a pastry blender or two knives to cut in the butter until the mixture forms coarse crumbs. Stir in the cream and egg. Turn out the dough onto a lightly floured surface and knead for about 2 minutes. Form into a ball and roll out to a ½-inch-thick sheet and cut into squares or biscuits. Place the shortcakes on baking sheets, evenly spaced about 2 inches apart.

Bake for 20 minutes, or until golden. Transfer the shortcakes to wire racks to cool completely. To serve, split each cake in half, top the bottom half with berries and whipped cream, if desired, and place the remaining half of the shortcake on top.

Texas Chocolate Sheet Cake

Serves 20

We have been to many barbecues where Texas Sheet Cake is the dessert of choice. Made with buttermilk, it's light, it's delicious—and it's chocolate.

CAKE

2 cups all-purpose flour

2 cups white cane sugar

1 teaspoon baking soda

1 teaspoon ground cinnamon

¼ teaspoon salt

¾ cup water

8 tablespoons (1 stick) unsalted butter, softened

¼ cup unsweetened cocoa powder

½ cup buttermilk

1 teaspoon vanilla extract

2 large eggs

ICING

6 tablespoons (¾ stick) unsalted butter, softened

⅓ cup whole milk or buttermilk

¼ cup unsweetened cocoa powder

2 teaspoons vanilla extract

3 cups confectioners' sugar, sifted

¼ cup chopped pecans, toasted

Preheat the oven to 375°F. Coat a 10 by 15-inch rimmed baking sheet with nonstick cooking spray and dust it with a little flour (about 2 teaspoons).

To make the cake, combine the flour, sugar, baking soda, cinnamon, and salt in a large bowl and whisk to blend. Combine the water, butter, and cocoa in a small saucepan and bring to a boil over medium heat, stirring frequently. Remove from the heat and pour into the flour mixture. Beat at medium speed until well blended. Add the buttermilk, vanilla, and eggs and beat well. Pour the batter into the prepared pan and bake for 15 to 20 minutes, or until a wooden toothpick inserted in the center comes out clean. Cool on a wire rack.

Make the icing while the cake is still hot: Combine the butter, milk, and cocoa in a medium saucepan and bring to a boil over medium heat, stirring constantly. Remove from the heat and stir in the vanilla and the confectioners' sugar, a little at a time, followed by the pecans. Spread over the hot cake. Cool completely on a wire rack before cutting and serving.

Note: You also can make this recipe in a 9 by 13-inch baking pan. Bake at 375°F for 20 to 25 minutes.

Kansas Dirt

Serves 10 to 12

This is a real winner. It helped Team Kansas City win two World Barbecue Championships in Ireland, in 1989 and 1990. It's also a winner at your backyard barbecue. Paul begged his wife, Jessica, to please give us the recipe.

1 (18-ounce) package Oreo cookies, crushed

1 (8-ounce) package cream cheese, softened

8 tablespoons (1 stick) unsalted butter

1 cup confectioners' sugar, sifted

3 cups whole milk

2 (3.4-ounce) packages instant vanilla pudding

1 teaspoon vanilla extract

1 (12-ounce) container frozen whipped topping

Spread half of the crushed cookies in the bottom of a 9 by 13-inch baking pan. With a mixer on medium speed, cream together the cream cheese, butter, and confectioners' sugar until smooth. Add the milk, pudding mix, vanilla, and whipped topping and blend well. Pour the mixture over the crushed cookies and top with the other half of the cookie crumbs. Freeze until firm, then cut into squares and serve.

Resources

Since ribs have been popular for decades, it is no surprise that rib resources abound. Here we offer a few of our favorites for rib information, inspiration, and entertainment. Our "rib radar" is always on. Turn yours on and you'll be surprised at how much rib stuff almost falls in your lap.

- **Brake for flea markets, garage sales, and estate sales:** One happy result of America's passion for accumulating stuff is that sooner or later people get rid of stuff to make room for more stuff. Sometimes that stuff includes old cookbooks or barbecue gadgets. If you're lucky, you'll find some good vintage rib recipes or perhaps a rib rack that is still good as new.

- **Grow and maintain your social network:** Exercise your interdependence. Once people know your passions, no matter what, they will call your attention to things, links, and people that they think you'll want to know about. Don't expect rib offerings, but you could find yourself becoming a pig magnet. We by all means recommend including butchers, meat cutters, backyard cooks, contest cooks, and professional pitmasters in your network.

- **Commit yourself to lifelong learning:** There is so much to learn and so little time. Don't let that stop you. Learn from books, from cooks, from friends, relatives, and strangers. And, especially when mastering rib cooking, learn by doing. Cooking is a mix of art, technique, and science. There's always more to learn, so take a class. And another and another.

Meat purveyors:

If you happen to be in Kansas City, you've got a lot of great choices for buying your ribs—five of our favorites are Scavuzzo's, Bichelmeyer Meats, Arrowhead Specialty Meats, KC Buffalo Company, and Dodge City Beef. Likewise, we recommend starting with your local butcher. It may require a special order. If your butcher gets bison ribs for you, be sure to bring him or her a sample of your smoked bison ribs. You could escalate local demand! If your butcher won't special order them, there are many online options. The best place to start is by checking the National Bison Association Buyer's Guide at www.bisoncentral.com/bison-buyers-guide, where you'll find sources from Waco to Wasilla and California to Maine.

Woods for smoking:

You can get wood chips and pellets from a number of online sources, including Amazon.com. Here are a few of our favorite sources:

Our longtime friend—and a competition cooker herself—Candy Weaver runs **BBQr's Delight** in Pine Bluff, Arkansas. It specializes in smoke-flavoring pellets and sells a lot of varieties. You can buy your pellets through the online store at bbqrsdelight.com, as well as view tips and instructional videos that'll convert you into what barbecuers call a "pellethead."

BarbecueGrillsAndMore.com is a great source for grills, smokers, other equipment, accessories, and all kinds of fuel, and the site is easy to search and navigate.

Charcoalstore.com is another great, easy-to-use site for all things grilling and barbecuing, including your chips, chunks, planks, and pellets. You even can search by species of wood.

Smoke 'n' Fire, **www.smokenfire.com**, offers everything you need for outdoor cooking, from equipment and fuel to rubs, sauces, books, DVDs, and more.

Helpful Web sites:

Putting *ribs* in your search engine will yield millions of links. As with all things Internet, you are left to your own judgment as to the value and reliability of findings. Here are a few we like.

Amazing Ribs, www.amazingribs.com. Craig Goldwyn has distinguished himself as the foremost go-to man for online rib information. His Web site is packed with recipes, information, inspiration, and entertainment. When we first met Craig years ago as judges at The Jack, we were impressed with his passion for barbecue, his background as a food and wine expert, and his congenial personality. We've been barbecue buddies ever since. Craig covers all the bases and continuously adds more content. A subscription to his online newsletter is free.

TheMeatSource.com, www.themeatsource.com/index.html, offers good basic information on meat selection, prep, doneness temperatures, and other online answers when you are in a hurry.

Interesting reads:

There are lots of great books on ribs and a few cookbooks. These are some of our favorite books that are a bit more obscure.

Barbecued Ribs and Other Great Feeds, by Jeanne Voltz (New York: Alfred A. Knopf, 1985); Knopf released a revised and expanded edition, ***Barbecued Ribs, Smoked Butts and Other Great Feeds***, in 1996. We recommend both. We like the original because there's nothing like the vintage edition. We like the revised for the extra recipes and expanded information. Although Jeanne died at the age of eighty-one in 2002, her barbecue legacy and influence continue today through these books and her many years as food editor for major newspapers and *Woman's Day* magazine.

Memphis Ribs, by Gerald Duff (Bend, Oregon: Salvo Press, 1999). Murder, Memphis in May, ribs, and Mississippi Delta blues are in good hands when Gerald Duff takes pen in hand. Not a cookbook, but a great source of barbecue entertainment and inspiration. Duff's descriptions of Memphis cuisine as he tells his tale always makes us hungry for Memphis-style baby backs, wet or dry.

Thin Blue Smoke, by Doug Worgul (London, Basingstock & Oxford: Pan Macmillan, 2009). At last a barbecue novel we can believe in! Don't miss Ms. Periwinkle Brown's description of Memphis wet ribs and dry ribs, but stick around for the whole story.

In her fascinating book on early American history, ***Creatures of Empire—How Domestic Animals Transformed Early America*** (Oxford: Oxford University Press, 2004), Virginia DeJohn Anderson explains why Native Americans didn't fit the "lazy" stereotype Europeans gave them for not domesticating animals such as bison. They used their knowledge of bison migration habits to harvest as many bison as needed. In addition, she points out that bison do not take well to confinement and that most bison meat today comes from bison-cattle hybrids, which are more amenable to domestication.

Acknowledgments

Throughout the writing and development of this book we tried to channel rib inspiration from a centuries-old line of ribmasters, past and present. Some we've acknowledged by name. Others we don't know by name, but we know we stand on their shoulders.

We are especially grateful for the patience and superb editing expertise of Lane Butler. She understands us, and gentle taskmaster that she is, brings out our best.

Dennis Hayes of BarnDance Productions, our agent, originated the idea for this book and, with his persistence, creativity, and enthusiasm, saw it through to fruition. We value his professionalism as well as his friendship.

The entire Andrews McMeel team has been a pleasure and an honor to work with. To Kirsty Melville, head of the book division; Tim Lynch and Diane Marsh, the design team; Tammie Barker, publicist, and the marketing team, we give our thanks and applause. Thanks to Jonathan Chester and Selma Dakota for the chapter opener photos.

Rib and recipe testers: Gretchen Davis, Jessica Kirk, David "ChopChopRubRub" Woosley, Howard Rasmussen, Jim Pipher, Linda Donnelly, Sarah and Alan Krause, Lee and Kelli Davis, Nancy Johnston, George and Loretta Reising, Billy Rodgers, Bob and Patti Stone, Russ Sifers, Tom and Judy Hyde, Robert and Gayle Krughoff, Ron and Joan Goettsch, Perry and Cheri Skrukrud, Lysa Allman-Baldwin, Don Lambert, Debbie Little-Wilson, Ron Osborne, Byron Long, Terri Yunghans, Paul and Tracy Satterfield, John Ross, CC Barton, Mary Fischer, Susan Hill, Jane Booth, Karlon Kruse, and Gordon Davis.

Inspiration, information, and encouragement: Gretchen Davis, Jessica Kirk, DennyMike Sherman, Kell Phelps, Lisa and Tom Raitt, Judith Fertig, Karen Adler, Carolyn Wells, Jill Silva, Ron Buchholz, Bill Herman, Brad and Kathy Sullivan, Barbara Ginsterblum, Neil Ginsterblum, Tana Shupe, Phil Litman, Susan Gordon, Josh Baum, John Scavuzzo of Scavuzzo's Meats, Phyllis Mueller, Mama Lew, Doug Worgul, George Dugger, Mary Winslow, Gloria Walker, Diane Thompson, Terry Lee, Steve Parman, Ann Davis, Lance Robertson, Amy Winn, Ann Rehnstrom, Toni Wellshear, Carla Ball, Carol Mohling, Charlie Loudon, Charlie Podrebarac, Chip Chapman, Ron Harwell, Craig Goldwyn, Dave Eckert, David Bailey, Thomas Snodell, David Emmott, John T. Strickland, Charles Striebinger, Wood Dickinson, Scott Cook, Pat "Tower Rock" Burke, John Willingham, Chris Schlesinger, Wayne Lohman, Bill Gage, Tony Stone, Mike Mills, Amy Mills, Dayna Chastain, Debbie Christian, Angelo Lucchesi, Jeff Arnett, Frank "Frog" Bobo, RD Davis, and Johnny White.

Storytellers: John Raven, Jessica Kirk, Mason Steinberg, Smoky Jon Olson, Clint Blackwell, Candy Weaver, Guy Simpson, Phil Litman, and Mike Lake.

Special thanks to Stan and Ann Nelson for the "best" story, and to Johnny White and his staff at Johnny's BBQ. Thanks to Michelle Holden and the staff at the Cedar-Roe Library for the meeting space, and to Guy Simpson and Jason Day for helping us make the food photos happen.

Metric Conversions and Equivalents

Approximate Metric Equivalents

VOLUME

¼ teaspoon	1 milliliter
½ teaspoon	2.5 milliliters
¾ teaspoon	4 milliliters
1 teaspoon	5 milliliters
1¼ teaspoon	6 milliliters
1½ teaspoon	7.5 milliliters
1¾ teaspoon	8.5 milliliters
2 teaspoons	10 milliliters
1 tablespoon (½ fluid ounce)	15 milliliters
2 tablespoons (1 fluid ounce)	30 milliliters
¼ cup	60 milliliters
⅓ cup	80 milliliters
½ cup (4 fluid ounces)	120 milliliters
⅔ cup	160 milliliters
¾ cup	180 milliliters
1 cup (8 fluid ounces)	240 milliliters
1¼ cups	300 milliliters
1½ cups (12 fluid ounces)	360 milliliters
1⅔ cups	400 milliliters
2 cups (1 pint)	460 milliliters
3 cups	700 milliliters
4 cups (1 quart)	0.95 liter
1 quart plus ¼ cup	1 liter
4 quarts (1 gallon)	3.8 liters

LENGTH

1/8 inch	3 millimeters
¼ inch	6 millimeters
½ inch	1.25 centimeters
1 inch	2.5 centimeters
2 inches	5 centimeters
2½ inches	6 centimeters
4 inches	10 centimeters
5 inches	13 centimeters
6 inches	15.25 centimeters
12 inches (1 foot)	30 centimeters

WEIGHT

¼ ounce	7 grams
½ ounce	14 grams
¾ ounce	21 grams
1 ounce	28 grams
1¼ ounces	35 grams
1½ ounces	42.5 grams
1⅔ ounces	45 grams
2 ounces	57 grams
3 ounces	85 grams
4 ounces (¼ pound)	113 grams
5 ounces	142 grams
6 ounces	170 grams
7 ounces	198 grams
8 ounces (½ pound)	227 grams
16 ounces (1 pound)	454 grams
35.25 ounces (2.2 pounds)	1 kilogram

Metric Conversion Formulas

TO CONVERT	MULTIPLY
Ounces to grams	Ounces by 28.35
Pounds to kilograms	Pounds by 0.454
Teaspoons to milliliters	Teaspoons by 4.93
Tablespoons to milliliters	Tablespoons by 14.79
Fluid ounces to milliliters	Fluid ounces by 29.57
Cups to milliliters	Cups by 236.59
Cups to liters	Cups by 0.236
Pints to liters	Pints by 0.473
Quarts to liters	Quarts by 0.946
Gallons to liters	Gallons by 3.785
Inches to centimeters	Inches by 2.54

Oven Temperatures

To convert Fahrenheit to Celsius, subtract 32 from Fahrenheit, multiply the result by 5, then divide by 9.

DESCRIPTION	FAHRENHEIT	CELSIUS	BRITISH GAS MARK
Very cool	200°	95°	0
Very cool	225°	110°	¼
Very cool	250°	120°	½
Cool	275°	135°	1
Cool	300°	150°	2
Warm	325°	165°	3
Moderate	350°	175°	4
Moderately hot	375°	190°	5
Fairly hot	400°	200°	6
Hot	425°	220°	7
Very hot	450°	230°	8
Very hot	475°	245°	9

Common Ingredients and Their Approximate Equivalents

1 cup uncooked rice = 225 grams

1 cup all-purpose flour = 140 grams

1 stick butter (4 ounces • ½ cup • 8 tablespoons) = 110 grams

1 cup butter (8 ounces • 2 sticks • 16 tablespoons) = 220 grams

1 cup brown sugar, firmly packed = 225 grams

1 cup granulated sugar = 200 grams

Information compiled from a variety of sources, including *Recipes into Type* by Joan Whitman and Dolores Simon (Newton, MA: Biscuit Books, 2000); *The New Food Lover's Companion* by Sharon Tyler Herbst (Hauppauge, NY: Barron's, 1995); and *Rosemary Brown's Big Kitchen Instruction Book* (Kansas City, MO: Andrews McMeel, 1998).

Index

D

E

F

G